autumn
LEAVES

God Bless You!
Russ Luver ?

autumn
LEAVES

A Collection of Scriptures, Meditations and Prayers

Russell J. Levenson, Jr.

Insight Press
Covington, Louisiana

Autumn Leaves: A Collection of Scriptures, Meditations and Prayers

Insight Press, Inc.
P.O. Box 5077, Covington, LA 70434
© 2017 by Insight Press
All rights reserved. First printing 2017.
Printed in the United States of America

Cover artwork by Russell J. Levenson, Jr., oil on canvas, *Falling Graces*.

All Scripture quotations, unless otherwise indicated, are taken from the New Revised Standard Version Bible, copyright © 1989, Division of Christian Education of the National Council of the Churches of Christ in the United States of America Used by permission. All rights reserved.

Every effort has been made to trace the owner or holder of each copyright. If any omissions have been made or any rights have been inadvertently infringed upon, we ask that the omission be excused and agree to make the necessary corrections at the earliest possible opportunity.

Library of Congress Control Number: 20179480/6

ISBN: 978–0–914520–67–2

Dedicated to

My wife, Laura, and family

with love and gratitude for their unending supply

of encouragement and support

and to the staff and members of St. Martin's Episcopal Church

with deep appreciation for their prayers, friendship and

the work of sharing the Gospel together.

CONTENTS

MEDITATIONS

A Word of Welcome

"You who live in the shelter of the Most High,
who abide in the shadow of the Almighty,
will say of the Lord, 'My refuge and my fortress;
my God, in whom I trust.'"

— Psalm 91:1-2

Here is the purpose for this book—*to give you a place of shelter in your daily life.* What follows is a set of meditations, inspired by selected Scriptures from the Old and New Testaments, with the hope that wherever you find yourself in your relationship with Jesus Christ, or the faith we followers of Jesus call "Christianity," you will come out at the book's end having given a portion of each day during the autumn season to time set aside with Him.

I don't know how you do that personally. I find that such reflection time for me is best in the morning—before the news is turned on or the email account is opened. I pour a cup of coffee, and try and give a portion of each morning to prayer, study and reflection. I am not always successful and often fail—but I do know when I do this I sense His presence more fully in the day that follows.

Let me tell you a bit about how this book is set up. I have written three other devotional books for three other seasons of the year:

Preparing Room, an Advent Companion for the winter season; *Provoking Thoughts,* for the Lenten season when winter gives way to spring; and *Summer Times,* for the slower and longer days of summer. And so *Autumn Leaves* is offered to round out this collection.

Like the others, each meditation has a title, followed by a scripture. In the first half of the book, scriptures are taken from the Hebrew Bible, or Old Testament, and in the second half, the scriptures come from the New Testament. If you are not a regular student of the Bible, I have tried, in most of the selected scriptures, to add a bit of background regarding the author of the chosen verses, the time in which it was written and a bit of context; perhaps this will encourage you to dig just a bit deeper into parts of the Bible that may be new to you.

Following the scripture, there is a meditation—most of which is based on the kinds of experiences and moments that occur during the fall season. At the close of each meditation there is a brief passage under the heading of *A New Leaf,* which specifically invites you to look at things with a different perspective, or maybe with just a fresh set of eyes. Finally, there is a prayer, either from the Christian tradition or my own hand. Keeping in mind that we don't all learn in the same way, you'll also note photos and illustrations carefully chosen to enhance each meditation. In addition, there is space in most meditations to write your own thoughts and reflections.

Some of the invitations are longer than others. The season of autumn is longer than 40 days, so you may want to move through the meditations at varying speeds—spending a day or more on one; and perhaps reading one or more on others. It is designed as a traveling companion—not a burdensome addition to your daily "to do" list.

It may seem obvious, but I am writing from the perspective of a Christian who came to faith in Christ in a particular way at a particular time in life. So, wherever you are in your relationship with God, or from whatever faith tradition you come—know that you have picked up a book offered from one who actually believes all the words I have included. I am honest enough to fully admit that I am on a journey and—as I will offer at the close of this work—I have so much yet to learn. But what I have now, I share with you.

In his book *The Case for Christianity*, C.S. Lewis offers some helpful breathing room for those inquiring into the Christian faith. He writes,

> I have been asked to tell you what Christians believe, and I am going to begin by telling you one thing that Christians don't need to believe. If you are a Christian you don't have to believe that all the other religions are simply wrong all through. If you are an atheist you do have to believe that the main point in all the religions of the world is simply one huge mistake. If you are a Christian, you are free to think that all these religions, even the queerest ones, contain at least some hint of the truth. When I was an atheist I had to try to persuade myself that the whole human race were pretty good fools until about one hundred years ago; when I became a Christian I was able to take a more liberal view. But, of course, being a Christian does mean thinking that where Christianity differs from other religions, Christianity is right and they are wrong. Like in arithmetic – there's only one right answer to a sum, and all other answers are wrong: but some of the wrong answers are much nearer being right than others.[1]

Autumn Leaves is offered as an attempt to help the reader get a bit deeper toward the truths that are offered in and through the Christian faith, and a life in and through Christ. My hope, and invitation, is that you simply come to it with an open heart and mind.

Some words of sincere thanks. A word of gratitude to my mentor, friend, publisher and former professor, the Reverend Dr. Fisher Humphreys, who has picked up this series of books and helped me in getting them into the hands of readers around the country. I thank Rebecca England, who performed the first round of edits and then handed the ball off to our St. Martin's Communications Department led by Karin Thornton, who oversaw final edits and production, Aleeta Bureau, who secured permissions and David Bolin, who worked tirelessly on the layout. I am also grateful to my faithful and extraordinarily helpful assistants at St. Martin's Episcopal Church, who also happen to be my colleagues and friends—Carol Gallion, Brittney Jacobson and Allie Hippard—who have also helped with editing, layout, and keeping the ball rolling so that the book

---

1   C.S. Lewis, *The Case for Christianity* (Nashville: Broadman & Polman Publishers, 1996), p. 31.

could be published and distributed in a timely manner. And to those who have kindly endorsed this book on the back cover—my profound gratitude.

I am grateful to the lay leadership of St. Martin's who have encouraged me to keep writing as a part of my ministry, and to the members of this remarkable Church family who understand that time writing often means time away from the office.

And lastly, and most especially, I offer my thanks to my wife, Laura—who remains the most honest and loving critic and cheerleader I have; a partner in life and ministry; and one with whom it is a profound honor to simply make our way through life together, in good times, bad and all in between; in whom I find joy in simply breathing the same air together.

And now, I invite you to turn this leaf in the book and begin your autumn journey—may it be a good journey, indeed.

A Prayer As You Begin

O Almighty God, Who pours out on all who desire it the spirit of grace and of supplication: Deliver us, when we draw near to You, from coldness of heart and wanderings of mind, that with steadfast thoughts and kindled affections we may be present before You, in spirit and in truth; through Jesus Christ our Lord. *Amen.*[2]

---

2   A Prayer Amended from "Before Worship," in *Prayer Book and Hymnal*, Charles Mortimer Guilbert, Custodian (New York: The Church Hymnal Corporation, 1986), p. 833.

A Change of View

*"And the Lord God made garments of skins for
the man and for his wife, and clothed them."*

— Genesis 3:21

I have a few kaleidoscopes that I keep near my desk. Sometimes, particularly when I have had a challenging conversation with someone where we might not have seen "eye to eye," I pick one up, hold it up to the light and give it a few turns. They are reminders to me that not everyone sees everything the same way—and in fact, sometimes the way I am seeing things needs a fresh perspective, a change of view.

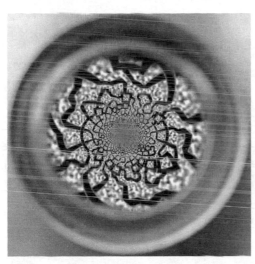

The first book of Scripture, Genesis, has much to offer. Its first phrase in Hebrew is *hereshith*, meaning "in the beginning." The English title we use comes from the Greek *geneseos*, which could have a variety of meanings—birth, origin, even genealogy. In any case, for those of us in Judeo-Christian faiths it is the starting point. We almost immediately think of that opening chapter of our story—creation born, flora and fauna come to life, man and woman brought to life by the breath, the *ruach*, of God. A good day or two, and then, well—the devil shows up and everything goes quickly down the drain. Temptation, deception, betrayal, shame, and ultimately punishment as Adam and Eve are banished from Eden. Onward.

But there is a kind of throwaway line in the story that many people miss. After Adam and Eve carry out the first "cover up," we are told,

[1] before they were tossed into the harsh cruel world, God sat down and made them garments to wear—He *"clothed them,"* the Scriptures say.

Does that not say a lot about God? He really is a parent. God certainly has days when He is angry at what His children have done, but that does not mean He stops loving them, caring for them, providing for them. Here, "in the beginning" sin was born (original sin we theologians call it); God could have wiped the blackboard clean and given it another start. But nope, He decided—even in the midst of the discipline He was about to carry out—not to send His children into the world without the protection they needed.

When this line caught my eye some years ago, it was a kaleidoscope moment. I often focused on the sin and guilt and shame and punishment part; and passed right over the truth that even then—in fact right in the middle of it—there was God's care. The psalmist would remind the reader, *"O give thanks to the Lord, for He is good, for his steadfast love endures forever."*[2] We do not dismiss what went wrong in Eden, but what if we also had a change of view and considered what went right? God did not stop the story when things got off to a rocky start—it just became part of the story—a story He actually plays a part in by revealing His intention to watch over His children and care for them, even when they stray from Him.

The reason I begin with this reflection is that I find in my work way too many people live in the past. They become weighed down with their guilt, sin, mistakes, bad decisions. When that becomes a part of who you are—grafted into your heart—then it can begin to define you. You have a myopic view that only sees the sin and it's easy to transfer that view onto how you believe God sees you.

1   William Blake, *The Angel of the Divine Presence Clothing Adam and Eve with Coats of Skins*, Object 3, 1803, 39.3 x 28.7 cm. © Fitzwilliam Museum, Cambridge / Art Resource, NY.
2   Psalm 136:1.

But give the kaleidoscope a turn or two, and remember that God is always making life out of mud pies, if we would but let Him. My hunch is the clothes God fashioned for Adam and Eve fit just right—perhaps God even took a step back after donning His firstborn creatures, with needle clinched between divine teeth, a smile and a pat and a "There...there...that ought to do it." Why would He do such a thing? It was His way of saying, "Let us get on with life—exhale the past, inhale the future." A change of view, indeed.

 ## A New Leaf

Do you need to turn over a new leaf when it comes to understanding God? None of us is perfect and certainly when we sin confession is good for the soul; but do we live in the past, or can we turn the past over and live into the present and future? When we hand over our dark places to God, He not only tosses them away (*"as far as the east is from the west, so far he removes our transgressions from us,"* the psalmist writes), but He also will *"cleanse us from all unrighteousness"* as the Apostle John would write—as if the past never happened at all.[3] In other words, God forgives the repentant sinner and He does not hold it against you—perhaps you should do the same to the one in the mirror. Perhaps you need a change of view.

A PRAYER

Lord, help me this day to give You the dark places in my heart and soul. As I do, give me the faith to hold fast to Your grace and mercy, which restore me to the child You created me to be. *Amen.*

---

3   Psalm 103:12; I John 1:9.

God in the Shadows

"God said, 'This is the sign of the covenant that I made
between me and you and every living creature that is with
you, for all future generations: I have set my bow in the
clouds, and it shall be a sign of the covenant between me
and the earth.'"

— Genesis 9:12–13

As the axis of the earth shifts, we begin to see longer shadows at day's end. Shadows that bespeak the coming of shorter days and longer nights. Sometimes long nights can be unnerving, frightening. Light and dark have always been metaphors for good and evil— Jesus' followers are often called the children of light, whereas Satan's minions are called children of darkness.[1]

It is, frankly, sometimes hard to see the light of God when the dark shadows of the world creep about us. I will not use this space to unfold some thoughts on the "whys" around the world's darkness; I will circle back to that later. But for now, no one could argue that we do not have great darkness, great evil in the world.

The story of Noah is known to every Christian from Vacation Bible School to adulthood. We tend to focus on all the good parts of the story—cute animals, two by two strutting into the protective ark with a small band of family members. We talk about the flood, but we usually do not bring up the fact that the 150 days of rain that flooded the face of the known earth was sent to wash away the evil of the world—that humans and animals were perishing in those flood waters. No, we lean in not to those unsavory parts of this story, but

---

1   See Ephesians 5:8, "For once you were darkness, but now in the Lord you are light. Live as children of light" and I Thessalonians 5:5, "for you are all children of light and children of the day; we are not of the night or of the darkness."

to the protection of God, the resting of the ark on Mount Ararat, the dove returning with an olive leaf as if to announce the good news that the waters were receding. And then, of course, there is the rainbow… God's promise that He will not use flood waters to cleanse the earth again.

At a distance, it is a good story— almost a fun story. Untold pounds of construction paper and crayons have been used by children to create happy memories about a God who protected Noah and the animals, and who protects us as well. But do we always feel protected? Do you? Do we, as God's children, wrestle with different kinds of darkness and wish sometimes that God would wipe away the evil in the world once more? I confess I do.

Many years ago, I was at a church convention in Shreveport, Louisiana, when I was called by a social worker friend to the hospital bed of a child who was facing certain death. I did not know the child, but he had been assigned to my friend and her care after he had been mercilessly beaten to the verge of death by his foster care father. She told me all of this before I came into the room, so I had a moment or two to digest it, but the moment I came in—the moment I saw that pitiful, swollen, bruised and frail little body, surrounded by weeping nurses and caretakers—my heart just broke...it broke to pieces.

I was told there was no chance that this child would live, but they wanted me to baptize him before they turned off any life support. We gathered our composure and began the service. Everyone was in prayer for this toddler. To this day, I will remember as I poured a bit of baptismal water on the forehead of that child, how one stream of the water ran down to the bridge of his nose, then to his closed eyelid and down his cheek—almost like a tear. We all saw it, and we all began to weep yet again. We prayed again, we hugged, but I left that hospital room utterly desolate.

As I came out to my car, I could hardly think clearly and a huge thunderstorm began; rain fell in thick sheets as I drove back to my hotel. It was raining so hard it was almost difficult to drive. As I made my way through the sheets of water, I began to weep again as I thought of that child. I confess, I was angry that our loving God could allow those kinds of things to happen in our world. Could He not have wiped out the abuser before he laid one hand on that child? I recall hitting the palms of my hands against the steering wheel and saying out loud, "Why, Lord? Why?"

I was truly at my wits' end. Please do not think I am trying to diminish one iota the horrible scene that still haunts me to this day, but after a while the rains began to subside. My car actually reached the top of a hill from which I had a fairly clear view of the entire downtown area and there—through my own tear-filled eyes—I saw a rainbow, a rainbow that literally stretched from one end of the city to the other. It remained in the sky through the rest of my drive. When I got back to my hotel, I told my wife about it and we pulled back the window blinds of our room. The rain had stopped and the rainbow was still there.

If I am honest, I do not know fully what all of that means; but I will take it for what it is worth. He sends beautiful sunsets over hospice wards, sunrises over battlefields and He sends rainbows—perhaps with the hope that what He sends will help mend our ways, or at the very least speak to our broken hearts; a reminder that even when the long shadows of darkness stretch over us, God is there.

A New Leaf

Read the paper, turn on the news, walk the streets of most inner cities—it is almost easy to believe that darkness is winning. But perhaps it is worth stepping back and looking where God might show up—even in dark places where He is least expected. Look for the rainbows.

A PRAYER

Sometimes, Lord, it is hard to believe.
I know, in my heart, You are good;
I know the great stories of our faith that tell how You watched over
and rescued Your children from danger and evil.
But when the long shadows creep over me,
it is hard to see anything but darkness,
and I wonder where You are...If You are...at all.

Give me faith Lord, to see when I am blinded by that darkness.
Give me light Lord, when evil seems to be at every turn.
Give me hope Lord, to trust and believe that even when all
seems lost,
You are still there.

God, please...please send me rainbows.
Amen.

Look Up

"He brought him outside and said, 'Look toward heaven and count the stars, if you are able to count them.' Then he said to him, 'So shall your descendents be.'

"And he believed the Lord; and the Lord reckoned it to him as righteousness."

— Genesis 15:5–6

One of the things about the shift from hot and humid summers (at least where I now live in Houston) to cooler, breezier falls, is that at night the stars and planets are more easily visible. I am no

astronomer, but in more than five decades of life I have spent a great deal of time outside at night looking at the stars—Orion's belt, Draco the Dragon, the Big and Little Dippers, the risings and settings of the moon, Venus, Mars. With a decent telescope, I have been able to spot the rings of Saturn, and the moons and great dark spot of Jupiter. There is much to see in looking up to the heavens—expanse is a good way to put it—an expanse that may make you feel rather small and insignificant.

It would be hard to write any set of reflections about God's dealings with us and leave out this crucial interchange between Abram and God.[1] You probably know the story. God has called Abram to leave

---

1   God has yet to rename Abram in this passage; this occurs in Genesis 17.

home and seek a promised land. Abram goes on nothing but a promise of God—a promise that if he goes, *"in you all the families of the earth shall be blessed."*[2] Whether that appealed to Abram's ego, or he just downright thought it best to go—because God was evidently setting the stage for something really big—we do not know. We do know that he went.

There were challenges along the way. There were dangers. By the time we get to this passage Abram is getting fearful. God must have sensed that fear and He says, *"Do not be afraid, Abram, I am your shield; your reward shall be very great."*[3]

You think that would be enough, but Abram presses it with God, because at this point he has no children…no one, should Abram die, to pass on this legacy God has promised. At this point, you can almost

see God shaking His divine head, putting an arm around good old Abram and saying, "Come outside with me. Look up at the stars. I created those, Abram—all of them. There are so many you cannot even count them. And if I can do that, I can do anything." It was almost as if God was playing coach to the fearful quarterback when the team is down and the fourth quarter is almost over. "Trust me now, Abram," God is saying. Abram, we are told *"believed,"* and that belief God credited to him as righteousness.

So we can see now why this passage is so important—it really is kind of ground zero of what it means to be a righteous person. Most of us tend to equate "righteousness" with being right all the time. Are any of us right all the time? Are you? I find I am wrong most of the time—and occasionally, somewhat right—but even then I question my motives.

The Scottish evangelist Henry Drummond once wrote, "Sin is a power in our life: let us fairly understand that it can only be met by another power."[4] I will write about this more as our autumn journey continues, but for now let us agree with Drummond. We usually know when

2   Genesis 12:3.
3   Genesis 15:1.
4   Henry Drummond, d. 1897.

we do not have it right and we often feel powerless to overcome our unrighteousness—so we need another power, outside of ourselves, to rescue us. We are not made holy and righteous because we try harder; we are made holy and righteous when we turn, "believe" (as Abram did) in God, trust in God—trust Him with our lives. In a word, being "righteous" is not so much about being right as it is about being right with God.

This is a crucial pill to swallow because our human tendency is to try harder, when what God is saying is "Trust in Me." If you are having a bit of trouble with that, take a moment tonight and if the sky is clear where you are, go outside…see the handiwork of God. If God can do that, think what He can do in you, with you, through you—let God whisper to you as He did to Abram, "Look up."

 A New Leaf

Of course one of the purposes of our faith is to empower us to live godly lives—lives that bespeak of the Holy Spirit of God working in and through us. Sadly, we too often think that's our work to do, when what we are called to do first and foremost is give our lives to God and let Him work in and through us. It really turns our human tendencies upside down, does it not? Perhaps it is time to focus not so much on being right, as on being right with God. How to do that? Look up, and believe, believe in Him.

A PRAYER

From deepest woe I cry to thee;
Lord, hear me, I implore thee!
Bend down thy gracious ear to me;
I lay my sins before thee.
If thou rememberest every sin,
if nought but just reward we win,
could we abide thy presence?

Thou grantest pardon through thy love;
thy grace alone availeth.
Our works could ne'er our guilt remove;
yea, e'en the best life faileth.
For none may boast themselves of aught,
but must confess thy grace that wrought
whate'er in them is worthy.

And thus my hope is in the Lord,
and not in my own merit;
I rest upon his faithful word
to them of contrite spirit.
That he is merciful and just,
here is my comfort and my trust;
His help I wait with patience.[5]
Amen.

— Martin Luther, d. 1546

---

5   Martin Luther (d. 1546), translated by Catherine Winkwork, (d. 1878). From *The Hymnal 1982* (New York: The Church Pension Fund, 1985), #151.

Even When We Grumble

"The Lord spoke to Moses and said, 'I have heard the complaining of the Israelites; say to them, 'At twilight you shall eat meat, and in the morning you shall have your fill of bread; then you shall know that I am the Lord your God.'"

— Exodus 16:11–12

I confess that I have been a grumbler from time to time. My grumbling is caused by lots of things—perhaps I did not get my way or got stuck in traffic. Sometimes it is when I am hungry, and if I am hungry and at a restaurant and I get an inattentive waiter—well, I grumble. I know people, and have prayed with a lot of them, who have much better reasons to grumble—they have cancer, or their marriage or a friendship is in serious trouble, maybe a child has run off the rails or one's job is in jeopardy. There are reasons to grumble. Some of them rather innocuous, but some downright appropriate.

For instance, in our lesson from the Hebrews we hear that "God hears" the grumbling of the Israelites and He sets out to do something about it. Some would say they had every right to grumble—at this part of the story, these descendants of Adam and Eve, the Hebrews, were rescued by a spirit-empowered Moses from years of toil and the burden of unceasing labor from dawn to dusk. They are on their way to a new land—that land flowing with milk and honey. Here we find them on

the fifteenth day of the second month after they departed Egypt—roughly 45 days in and the grumbling starts.

Why? Well they are in the desert—food is short. Have you ever been around kids late in the

12

day between lunch and snack time? It was probably something like that, except it is thousands of kids at the same time. The grumbling gets so bad some begin to say it would have been better to have died under whips, eating the food fit for slaves, than to continue on this journey through the desert to the promised land! But in their grumbling, they are forgetting; God has a hand in all of this, God is going to care for them—even when they grumble.

Given what He had done (plagues, parting sea and such) God might have chosen a bit of smiting. Certainly Moses, who had been head coach in this operation, might have reached his wits' end. You can almost see him rolling his eyes. You can see Aaron, his brother, setting up the microphone and lectern for God's updated message, "I've about had it with you folks, go back to Egypt, go back to slavery, I'm passing my expectations on to someone else...forget being the chosen people, I'm choosing a better lot."

Nope, God sticks with the grumblers—in fact, He says, "Come morning, I'm going to rain down bread from heaven. I'm going to take care of you. In the evening, quail will come—enough quail to capture, eat and get you through the day, and in the mornings, I'm going to send bread...bread from heaven. It will be white and taste wonderful..."

"This is bread that you can eat, but if you try and hoard it—try and keep more than your share or store it up—it will rot. It is bread that only lasts the day because it's more than bread. It's a symbol—let's call it 'daily bread'—a reminder that you and I have a relationship, and that despite your grumbling, despite forgetting that I'm the One who got you out from under Pharaoh's grip in the first place, I'm not pitching in the towel. You are still my children."[1]

---

1   Exodus 16:11–31; I have paraphrased a bit here.

13

Grumbling can serve a purpose. It helps us get things off our chest, but you and I both have met those folk who are perpetual grumblers—nothing is ever right. They are the kind of people who always see the glass as half full, can quickly find the one chink in the armor, the one hair that is out of place. I have worked with so many adults who suffered under the harsh grumbling of parents who never believed their children were up to par, employees who suffered under the weight of a grumbling boss, and so on.

You know that kind of grumbling can build a moat—a moat that others prefer not to cross, a moat that keeps God at arm's length. If nothing's ever right, well then I can live in my own little world, arms crossed, eyes down—forgetting, as the Hebrews had, that God was not giving up on them.

Santa may know when you are naughty or nice, but God cares for you when you are both. He cares for you even when you grumble. So God broke through the grumbling with a gift—a reminder—that they were His people and He was their God, and that even when things looked at their worst, He was not going to leave them to their own designs—a life of endless grumbling. That bread, which they called manna, broke through their grumbling and fed not just their stomachs, but their souls. It was an invitation to turn from griping about what they did not have, to embracing what they did—the constant and abiding presence of God.

What if God only cared for us when we had our act together? What kind of God would that be? No, the fact that we have a God who cares when we do not, says much more. The Venerable Fulton John Sheen, an American bishop of the Catholic Church, once wrote, "God does not love us because we are valuable. We are valuable because God loves us." That is what those Hebrews learned in the desert. It is a lesson worth clinging to—especially when we find ourselves grumbling.

A New Leaf

You may have something about which to grumble today—but has grumbling become a way of life? Do you feel like you are always getting a raw deal? The short end of the stick? Perhaps it is time to turn that leaf over—consider instead that God cares for you and loves you even in the midst of your grumbling. No doubt, if you spend some time feasting on the truth of that love, you will soon find your grumbling gone and your soul fed.

A Prayer

Lord Jesus, even You had days when You grumbled—at the bickering of Your disciples, the lack of faith of Your followers, religionists who turned Your Father's house into a den of thieves. I thank You for loving me, even when I grumble. But help me such that my life is more than a basket full of lament. Give me eyes that see Your hand at work in the world around me, and an open heart to allow Your love to so fill me that what I offer You, and the world, is not my perpetual grumblings, but the very joy of heaven. *Amen.*

The Right Way

"You shall not take vengeance or bear a grudge against any of your people, but you shall love your neighbor as yourself: I am the Lord. You shall keep my statutes."

— Leviticus 19:18–19

The book of Leviticus is essentially about holiness, but includes a great number of do's and don'ts. It includes a lot of laws. When I am encouraging a person to begin reading the Bible for the first time, I often say, "Don't start with Leviticus." It is long, a bit tedious, and lots of the do's and don'ts do not apply to our time and our day.

Please do not misunderstand me; I am not one who encourages (or buys into) situational ethics or moral relativity. There are some of God's laws that are, well, just beyond shifting given the circumstances (the Ten Commandments for starters).[1] But for this meditation, let me borrow some wisdom from Frederick Buechner,

> Law. There are basically two kinds: (1) law as the way things ought to be, and (2) law as the way things are. An example of the first is "No trespassing." An example of the second is the law of gravity.
>
> God's Law has traditionally been spelled out in terms of category No. 1, a compendium of do's and don'ts. These do's and don'ts are the work of moralists and when obeyed serve the useful purpose of keeping us from each other's throats. They can't make us human but they can help keep us honest.
>
> God's Law *in itself,* however, comes under category No. 2 and is the work of God. It has been stated in eight words: "He who does not love remains in death." (1 John 3:14)

---

1 Exodus 20:1–17.

Like it or not, that's how it is. If you don't believe it, you can always put it to the test just the way if you don't believe the law of gravity, you can always step out a tenth-story window.[2]

Many of us tend to associate "laws" with "restrictions." Some of them may seem like useless bother in our day-to-day lives (the speed limit for instance, or a stop sign on an empty street, or taxes for that matter). One could argue a lifetime over those kinds of laws. But notice in the passage above from Leviticus that set in the midst of lots of do's and don'ts are two key imperatives, *"Love your neighbor"* and *"Keep my statutes."*

When Jesus was once asked, "What is the greatest commandment?" He drew from this teaching as well as what our Jewish friends call the Shema from Deuteronomy.[3] His answer was simple, *"He answered, 'You shall love the Lord your God with all your heart, and with all your soul, and with all your strength, and with all your mind; and your neighbor as yourself.'"*[4] His answer was *love.*

Laws can be broken. You can run the red light, text while you drive or cheat on your taxes. You can lust after one who is married to another, steal from your neighbor, and you do not "have" to love anyone, but you would be breaking the law—moral laws and God's laws.

All those do's and don'ts in the Bible that essentially have to do with not harming others or yourself—well, really they are about something I pointed to a moment ago—holiness. Not holiness in a sense of perfection, but holiness in the sense of wholeness, of being

2   Frederick Buechner, *Wishful Thinking* (San Francisco: HarperSanFrancisco, 1973), pp. 50–51.
3   Deuteronomy 6:4–5.
4   Luke 10:27; cf. Mark 12:30–31; Matthew 22:37–39.

completely at peace with God and others. The best way to do that is to live into the two great laws—that vertical law of loving God and that horizontal law of loving others.

Arthur Michael Ramsey, 100th Archbishop of Canterbury, wrote, "The essence of the ethics of Jesus is not law, but a relationship of persons to God." Rather than see law as an intrusion, what if we saw it as simply the right way to live? The most right way is a right relationship and the most right relationship is that of love—love of neighbor, of self, of God. That is what makes us right; that is what makes us holy; that is the law of God—and it is the right way to live.

 A New Leaf

Where might God's laws seem like an intrusion into your life? What if you turned the way of seeing such intrusion instead as an invitation? An invitation to a better life? A more holy life? A more whole life? An invitation that begins merely with a willingness to be loved by God and to love Him in return and thereby be empowered to love all who come your way—even yourself? Welcome His law of love and know His peace.

A PRAYER

O Lord, rescue me from myself
and give me unto you.
Take away from me all those things
that draw me from you
and give me those things
that lead me to you.
Amen.

— Eric Abbott, d. 1983

Self-Sinking

*"Now the man Moses was very humble, more so
than anyone else on the face of the earth."*

— Numbers 12:3

I suppose I have read the above passage several times over the years,
but not until I began this book did it really strike out at me. *"Moses was
very humble."* Leader...yes. Lawgiver...of course. Abolitionist without
compare...certainly. But humble? It is hard to think on that image
the late actor Charlton Heston gave us of Moses, standing tall before
the soon-to-be-parted Red Sea and telling the Hebrews to "behold the
hand of God," and couple that with humility. Yet we are told here,

he was, in fact, more
humble than anyone
on planet earth.

We preacher types
often decry the decay
of culture with words
like "there used to be a
time when..." It would
be tempting to suggest
that we live in a time
when humility seems
not to be prized, but to
be shunned. I suppose that has always been the case. We tell stories
about heroes' great accomplishments. We cherish wins, trophies and
prizes. When it comes to college football games that crank up during
this season of the year, at the end of the game, it is the "most valuable
player" who is heralded, not the humblest one.

But you and I worship a God who turns most things on their head.
For instance, a foundational character trait of Jesus' followers was

to be humble. *"For all who exalt themselves will be humbled, and those who humble themselves will be exalted,"* Jesus offers.[1] Of course Jesus lived that humility right up to His last breath. As Paul reminds us, Jesus *"humbled himself and became obedient to the point of death—even death on a cross."*[2] The Apostle Peter called on the earliest Christians to *"clothe yourselves with humility in your dealings with one another, for 'God opposes the proud, but gives grace to the humble.'"*[3]

Humility is an odd trait because it requires that one step away from oneself, which would suggest you or I have to in some way "try" to be humble—as if it is a contest…which seems to run quite upstream to humility itself! A "most humble" award would be rather ironic. How do we attain it?

A primary step is simply to get yourself out of the way—out of the way of others, yourself—out of the way of God. Taking a step back from the front of the line will enable us to be better used by God. If my first priority is myself, then, of course, everyone and everything else comes in second and third and fourth place, and so on. If I step back from myself, then it opens the possibility that someone or something else, which has little to do with what I want, blossoms. That is particularly true if we want to be used by God to advance His presence in this world and to serve His children around us.

Moses was a great man, but he was humble. He knew (and learned throughout life's journey) that God's will and way were more important than his. The end result? A nation of people was freed and given a new home away from captivity. I once read humility is not thinking less of yourself, it is thinking of yourself less.

The word "humility" actually comes from the Latin *humilitas,* a derivative of sorts from the adjective *humilis,* which means not only humble, but also "from the earth" or "ground." A close relative of the word is "humus," which is the dark organic matter we find in soil. Humus is essential to the health of other plants; in fact, the life of other plants depends on humus. Interestingly enough, however, it is composed in large part from the decay (death) of plant matter. This death of life makes way for more life.

As we step from season to season, as summer gives way to autumn, life continues. If summer had cognitive ability, we might say that it knows

---

1   Luke 14:11.
2   Philippians 2:8.
3   I Peter 5:5; cf. Proverbs 3:34.

its place. When it is time to yield to the fall, it humbles itself. Few are more readily identified with humility than Mother Teresa. This small nun of Calcutta could be tending to the wounds of the horrifically impoverished one day and addressing a joint session of Congress the next, yet she maintained that Christ-like quality of humility. She once said, "If you are humble, nothing will touch you, neither praise nor disgrace, because you know what you are."

In the end, humility is not so much something one achieves, but rather simply receives by stepping aside for others, and for Christians, for Christ Himself to rule in our hearts. C.H. Spurgeon, a 19th century English Baptist preacher, said, "The way to rise in the kingdom is to sink in ourselves."

Great things can happen when we yield to God's power. Moses freed a nation; Mother Teresa founded a home for the poor known round the world. But neither would have happened without humility, without stepping aside from their agenda and giving way to God's. As summer yields to fall so that the rich buffet of colors spring to life, when we yield to God His life grows larger still. Perhaps it's time to consider a bit of self-sinking.

A New Leaf

Spend a moment or two honestly thinking on your own humility. What are some concrete steps you could take to step back from what you want so that others can be blessed? What are ways you can more faithfully yield to Jesus so that He can work His will through you?

A PRAYER

Lord, let me live from day to day,
In such a self-forgetful way,
That even when I kneel to pray,
My pray'r shall be for OTHERS.

Help me in all the work I do
To ever be sincere and true,
And know that all I'd do for you
Must needs be done for OTHERS.

Let "Self" be crucified and slain
And buried deep, nor rise again
And may all efforts be in vain
Unless they be for OTHERS.

So when my work on earth is done,
And my new work in heav'n's begun,
May I forget the crown I've won,
While thinking still of OTHERS.

Yes, others, Lord, yes others,
Let this my motto be;
Help me to live for others,
That I may live like Thee.
Amen.

— Charles D. Meigs, d. 1869

Tending to the Garden

"Hear, O Israel: The Lord is our God, the Lord alone.
You shall love the Lord your God with all your heart,
and with all your soul, and with all your might."

— Deuteronomy 6:4

Are you a gardener? I am a bit of an amateur. My wife is leagues beyond my capabilities, but I do have a particular few items in our yard to which I tend. At summer's end, things need to be done to tend to the garden.

For instance, I grow peppers, but we had a lot of rain this summer, and too much rain does not make for healthy pepper plants. In years past, I have merely cut them back for the following year's growth.

This year, I just pulled out the unhealthy plants and tossed them away. There were other plants in the yard that—as annuals—had come to their natural end and they too needed to be uprooted and tossed. To make the garden flourish in the next season of its life, some things simply needed to be rooted out.

Idolatry, the worship or devotion of one's life to anything that would supplant God, is one thing that is most consistently condemned throughout the Judeo-Christian story. This passage from Deuteronomy is somewhat of God's "one-liner" about His rightful place in the hearts of His children. Written about 1400 B.C. after

23

the Exodus from Egypt and before entrance into the Promised Land, most of the book is simply a long reminder of Moses to the Israelites about all that God has done for them, all God is doing for them and all He wants to do for them. In return, they should constantly be on guard about allowing anything or anyone to take His place.

Now we sometimes see that as a negative. God is occasionally described as a "jealous God," desiring no competition for His rightful place in our lives.[1] But is God jealous for His sake or for our own? The testimony of Scripture would be that God is not trying to squelch us by restricting our worship and devotion to Him, and Him alone—but really trying to benefit us. Why? Because putting anything in God's place drives us away from Him and what He wants for us.

Blaise Pascal, a famous French mathematician and philosopher, put it like this: "What is it, then, that this desire and this inability proclaim to us, but that there was once in man a true happiness of which there now remain to him only the mark and empty trace, which he in vain tries to fill from all his surroundings, seeking from things absent the help he does not obtain in things present? But these are all inadequate, because the infinite abyss can only be filled by an infinite and immutable object, that is to say, only by God Himself."[2]

If we try to stuff anything but God into that God-shaped hole in our lives, we find ourselves discontented and dissatisfied. A passion for God is diluted with other things, and so the fullness of God cannot be experienced. But if we pour into Pascal's "God-shaped hole" God, our lives begin to take on an order that results in spiritual health, the fruit of abandoning idolatry.

1   See Exodus 34:14; Deuteronomy 4:24.
2   Blaise Pascal, *Pensées* (New York: Penguin Books, 1966), p. 75.

C.S. Lewis speaks to this as well. "God made us: invented us as a man invents an engine. A car is made to run on petrol, and it would not run properly on anything else. Now God designed the human machine to run on Himself. He Himself is the fuel our spirits were designed to burn, or the food our spirits were designed to feed on. There is no other. That is why it is just no good asking God to make us happy in our own way...God cannot give us a happiness and peace apart from Himself, because it is not there."[3]

Notice the brief title of this meditation, "Tending to the Garden." The likelihood is that all of us struggle with idolatry—and I suspect Pascal, Lewis and good old Moses did as well. So, it is less of a once and for all kind of practice, and more of a once, and again, and again. This fall, I had to get out there in my garden and uproot some things for the sake of a healthier garden. When it comes to tending the soul that is your garden, what might need rooting out? Tend to your garden.

 ## A New Leaf

Moses put it out there *"Love God with all of your heart...soul and strength."* Our Jewish friends call this the great Shema. It serves as a centerpiece of their morning and evening worship. Moses did not cut any corners—Love God with all, means all—and it does not mean some or most. Use a moment or two to acknowledge what might be getting in the way of that "all," and then ask God to help you root it out—better yet, ask Him to do the work. He is the better gardener!

A PRAYER

O Lord, let me not henceforth desire health or life, except to spend them for you, with you, and in you. You alone know what is good for me; do, therefore, what seems best to you. Give to me, or take from me; ...and may equally adore all that comes to me from you; through Jesus Christ our Lord.
Amen.

— Blaise Pascal, d. 1662

---

3   C.S. Lewis, *Mere Christianity* (New York: HarperCollins, 1980). p. 50.

Stepping Out in Faith

"When the soles of the feet of the priests who bear the ark of the Lord, the Lord of all the earth, rest in the waters of the Jordan, the waters of the Jordan flowing from above shall be cut off; they shall stand in a single heap."

— Joshua 3:13

When I was a kid growing up in Alabama, one of the great things about fall was raking up the leaves into a pile and then jumping in! I did this with my siblings and friends. Looking back now, it was interesting to see the variety of ways that jumping in was approached. I had some

friends who would literally dive in headfirst. I was a bit more timid and cautious. I once remember one friend who dove in and unfortunately landed on a hard rock below—not much fun in that. Some, perhaps only a few, were reluctant to jump in at all—not knowing what that leap might mean.

The snippet from Joshua above is a kind of turning point in the history of the Hebrew people. (I would bid you to pause here and read all of Chapter Three.) In sum this is what happens: we find the Hebrew people invited to pass through some water—the Jordan. Of course, it is not the first time they have been asked to do this; that was on the banks of the Red Sea when Moses lifted up his staff and they scurried through the walled-up waters with Pharaoh's soldiers nipping at their heels. This scene is about 40 years later. After wandering in the wilderness, making laws, breaking them, and being refined again and again by God's hand, the Hebrews are about to make a journey

26

from desert into the Promised Land. Moses is dead, leaving them in Joshua's charge and then they hit a snag—a big one.

They come to the edge of the Jordan River—not a trickling Jordan—a river at flood stage. They are going to have to go through the waters again; but this time, God will not do it alone. This time, they are called on to do their part.

Joshua gathers the people the next morning and tells them they are to put their eyes on the Levite priests, who will lift the ark and carry it down to the edge of the Jordan. Then he says, *"...By this you shall know that among you is the living God...When the soles of the feet of the priests who bear the ark of the Lord...rest in the waters of the Jordan, the waters of the Jordan flowing from above shall be cut off; they shall stand in a single heap."*[1]

That is exactly what happened, we are told—the sun rose, they broke camp and went down to the water's edge. The priests hoisted the ark, the visible sign of God's presence in their midst, and walked to the water's edge. Nothing happened—nothing at all—*until...*they stepped out and placed their foot into the water. At that moment, the water stopped, the Hebrews left the past, and stepped, literally, into

---

1   Joshua 3:10, 13.

27

the future. They came into the Promised Land because they followed, and in the end, because they chose to step out in faith. It's not what they did that enabled them to come into their new home, it was their belief in God—their faith, if you will, that made them put one foot in front of the other.

It really is a great story about taking a leap of faith—literally. So often we tend to hold back from things we think God might be calling us to do because we are afraid to step out in faith. We know God works in all kinds of ways. For instance, He does many things for us every day about which we have no say whatsoever. (What if you were responsible for making sure your heart beat at regular intervals?) While God may be watching over us, some things He allows us to do on our own. Some things, it seems, He wants to do "with us," to partner with us if you will—and so before venturing further He may suggest we take the first step—and then He will do the rest.

Practically, what might that mean? Have you felt God calling on you to do something of late and you have been putting it off because you do not know what would happen should you give it a try? In what way today are you being asked to step into the water and see what God will do through you? Perhaps you are feeling tension in a relationship with a friend, and need to pick up the phone and talk. Maybe there's a coworker you distrust, but could get to know better over coffee. It could be that your neighborhood is full of isolated and lonely people and God is leading you to reach out to them.

On a more personal level, maybe it is time to see what life is like without the burden of addiction. Maybe it is time to let go of a destructive or abusive relationship. Maybe it is time to quit making excuses for not praying, or not resting, or not laughing, or not crying, or not being more loving to the one or ones God has given you, or not doing the things God gave you the means to do.

Just put one foot into the water. I like what Dr. Martin Luther King, Jr., said, "You don't have to see the whole staircase, just take the first step." You don't have to see where the journey will end, just let it begin.

You know, usually—almost always really—once my friends and I took that leap into that pile of leaves it was a lot of fun, more fun than we probably could have imagined. It was worth that leap of faith. Today, stepping out in faith might be as well.

A New Leaf

My hunch is you already know what God is calling on you to do—
what step of faith He is asking you to take. If God is calling you to do
so...why wait? Take that first step...today...right now.

A PRAYER

O Savior Christ, who leads to eternal blessedness those who commit
themselves to you: grant that we, being weak, may not presume to
trust in ourselves, but may always have you before our eyes to follow
as our guide: that you, who alone knows the way, may lead us to
our heavenly desires. To you, with the Father and the Holy Spirit, be
glory forever. *Amen.*

— Miles Coverdale, d. 1568

The Way of Faithfulness

*"But Ruth said, 'Don't press me to leave you or to turn
back from following you! Where you go, I will go; where
you lodge, I will lodge; your people shall be my people,
and your God my God.'"*

— Ruth 1:16

I mentioned earlier that I grew up in Alabama. Stop your average
Alabamian on the street as autumn approaches and ask what they
are thinking about come Saturdays in the fall—most will respond,
"Football!" In Alabama, most will be speaking about their loyalty to

Alabama or Auburn. I have
also lived in Florida where
the answer would be the
University of Florida or Florida
State. I now live in Texas, and
your average Texan would
say The University of Texas,
Texas A&M University, Texas
Christian University or Baylor
University! Loyalty to a team
can be found in most places
across the United States. People—even people who have no formal
association with a football team—take great pride in putting up yard
flags, having bumper stickers on their cars, and wearing jerseys and
hats that visibly proclaim their loyalty to their team!

The book of Ruth is, essentially, about loyalty. The Gentile Ruth
marries into a Jewish family. When all of the men in the family die,
no one would have been surprised if Ruth decided to go her own way.
Her mother-in-law, Naomi, actually encourages her to go back to her
people, but Ruth is loyal and, as we see in this verse, she pledges to

go with Naomi—to stay with her, and be loyal to the family that took her in and to their God as well.

I could run down a few rabbit trails on this one, but let me limit myself to two. The first has to do with loyalty to those God has given to us in our relationships—friends and family. There is no question that there are people in our lives who may test our loyalty to them. An important caveat—there is no requirement to stick with someone who might bring harm or destruction into your life. But, when God brings people into our lives and when the bonds of affection in whatever form have been born, we are called to stick with those loved ones through thick and thin. In the marriage service, we ask a couple if they will stay loyal in all kinds of circumstances— "for better for worse, for richer for poorer, in sickness and in health."[1] There are things that certainly test that loyalty, but we are called to stand that test of time.

The second rabbit trail would be our loyalty to our faith. We express that in all kinds of ways, but in the same way our relationships can be tested, so can our relationship with our Church, and frankly, even our faith. Some years ago, a friend of mine was having a conversation with a Russian Christian who was staying with a family in Birmingham, Alabama, for a semester of study abroad. One day the young student said, "What I have found fascinating in your culture is that people seem to have no problem changing from one church to another, but they would never change allegiance to their football team!"

Of course, in a word, this comes down to faithfulness. St. John Chrysostom, once preached, "Faithfulness in little things is a big thing."[2] So true, do you not think?

Ruth set a wonderful standard for familial faithfulness and for faithfulness to God. The road she took is worth considering. If a football team is worthy of your devotion, would you not agree that those whom God has poured into your life deserve much more?

1   "The Celebration and Blessing of a Marriage," in *The Book of Common Prayer* (New York: The Church Hymnal Corporation, 1979), p. 427.
2   Died in 407.

When it comes to our allegiance to God, and to His family the Church, what better model than Jesus, about whom Oswald Chambers once wrote, "Watch where Jesus went. The one dominant note in his life was to do his Father's will. His is not the way of wisdom or of success, but the way of faithfulness." As our forebears would say, "Amen, so be it."

 ## A New Leaf

Football games are great. I have sat through more than I can count and cheered my teams on like the next guy. But the exuberance some show about their favorite sports team begs the question as to whether they can stir their hearts with a like—or better yet, more intense— passion for the loved ones in their lives? For their God? Does any of this speak to where you are today? Might Ruth's faithfulness inspire you to consider your own? What might you do differently today to be more faithful to your relationships? To your God?

A PRAYER FOR FAITHFULNESS TO FRIENDS...

Help me, O God, to be a good and true friend:
to be always loyal and never to let my friends down,
Never to talk about them behind their backs in a way which I
      would not do before their faces;
never to betray a confidence or talk about the things about which
      I ought to be silent;
always to be ready to share everything I have;
to be as true to my friends as I would wish them to be to me.
This I ask for the sake of him who is the greatest and truest of all
      friends, for Jesus' sake.
Amen.

— William Barclay, d. 1978

A Prayer for Faithfulness to God...

Now it is you alone that I love,
You alone that I follow,
You alone that I seek
You alone that I feel ready to serve,
because you alone rule justly.
It is to Your authority alone that I want to submit.
Command me, I pray, to do whatever You will,
But heal and open my ears
that I may hear your voice.
Heal and open my eyes
that I may see Your will.

Drive out from me
All fickleness,
that I may acknowledge you alone.
Tell me where to look
that I may see you,
and I will place my hope in doing your will.
Amen.

— St. Augustine, d. 430

Speak...For Your Servant Is Listening...

"...And Samuel said, 'Speak, for your servant is listening.'"

— I Samuel 3:10

There is something about the sound of leaves rustling in this season of the year—do you not agree? It is not the same sound wind makes when it blows through during winter when there are no leaves,

spring when the leaves are nimble and small, or in the summer when they are full grown. There is something different in the fall—have you listened lately?

Listening is hard—the world is full of distractions (when is the last time you looked at your cell phone?) and full of sounds (is your television on? Radio?). We hear lots of things on any given day, but how do we listen for the voice of God? One way is to make the space and time for that to happen. Samuel did that.

I Samuel was probably written by an unnamed author between 1100 and 1000 B.C. Most of its 31 chapters are about Israel's 12 tribes uniting under one king. How did that come about? Well, it happened because Samuel listened.

The whole of the story is found from I Samuel Chapters 1–3. But the short version is this—Samuel's mother, Hannah, prayed that she might conceive a son with her husband, Elkanah. When her prayer was answered, she named her boy Samuel, saying, "Because I asked the Lord for him." Samuel sounds much like the Hebrew word for

34

"heard of God." There is a lot of listening going on here. She was so grateful for her son that she dedicated him to the Lord and service in the temple of the Lord under the mentorship of the priest Eli.

One night as Samuel lay down to sleep, he heard a voice calling his name. He ran to Eli and said, *"Here I am...you called me."* Eli responded, *"I did not! Go lie back down."* This happened twice more before Eli sensed what was happening. *"Go lie down, and if you hear this again, say 'Speak, Lord, for your servant is listening.'"* Well, the rest is history—literally. God called Samuel to an incredible task and his life was changed forever, as was the nation of Israel. Here was the birthplace of the new way God's kingdom was going to run. It was not just a moment, but an invitation to enter a partnership with God to lead the Hebrew people. Samuel would not have known if he did not first hear God, and then, even more, invite God to speak because he was ready to listen. And, of course, Samuel would have to rely on that hearing and listening the rest of his life, as he anointed Saul to be king, and later, anointed the greatest king in Israel's history—David.

To be quiet, to listen, to be still—it is so hard. Recall the words of Psalm 46:10, *"Be still, and know that I am God!"* There are a number of reasons why we should be still and listen. The first reason we are called to be still, in part, is to remind us that we are "not God." A second reason we are called to be still is to connect to God. A third reason to be still is to become the people God calls us to be. That is precisely what happened when Samuel got still, was quiet and listened to the voice of God.

The sound of leaves in the fall is unlike their sound any other time of year. The sound of God's voice—in the still, small, quiet moments—is unlike any word our busy, full, loud, distracting world may offer us.

Perhaps make just a little extra time today. Turn off all the sounds of this world—go outside—listen. Before you do, pray, *"Speak Lord, for your servant is listening."* God knows what you may hear.

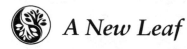 *A New Leaf*

Spend a moment or two and do an inventory of your day-to-day life. How much time do you spend listening for the voice of God? Is there one thing—just one—you could cut from your own schedule that might make more space for His voice?

A Prayer

Ah Lord, unto whom all hearts are open, You can govern the vessel of my soul far better than I can. Arise, O Lord, and command the stormy wind and the troubled sea of my heart to be still, and at peace in you, so that I may look up to you undisturbed, and abide in union with you, my Lord. Let me not be carried here and there by wandering thoughts; but, forgetting all else, let me see and hear you. Renew my spirit; kindle in me your light, that it may shine within me, and my heart may burn in love and adoration towards you. Let your Holy Spirit dwell in me continually, and make me your temple and sanctuary, and fill me with divine love and light and life, with devout and heavenly thoughts, with comfort and strength, with joy and peace. *Amen.*

— Johann Arndt, d. 1621

Giants Don't Have the Last Word

"But David said to the Philistine, 'You come to me with sword and spear and javelin; but I come to you in the name of the Lord of hosts...'"

— I Samuel 17:45

New beginnings are great—always a chance for a fresh start. But sometimes new beginnings are weighty. When fall comes, for many the lightness of summer gives way to the enormity of what follows. The year-end numbers are closer than they were back in January. We cram not one, but several holidays into the months ahead, the home may need to be readied for cooler temperatures, and so on. For a good bit of my adult life, I was a parent of children who were off to school as summer ended. There was always a good bit of stress and strain around that—even more so when they left home for college. For some of us it may just be overwhelming, beyond our capacity to defeat the giant tasks before us.

There is no better story in the Bible about defeating giants than the well-known combat between David and Goliath. You know the story. The Philistines and Israelites were at battle, but the Philistines' best tactic was not warfare, it was fear. They sent out Goliath of Gad, who was, by all accounts, about nine feet tall—think Yao Ming on steroids. For 40 days

(which is the Bible's way of saying "a long time"), like the bully on the playground, Goliath would come out and taunt not only the Israelites, but also their God.

But Goliath was a giant, and his stature alone was the source of the Israelites' reluctance to take him on. In stepped David...young David, from field of sheep to field of battle. He refused armor, and armed with only a sling shot and five stones, he stepped out to the disdainful sarcasm of the giant.

David knew he was not alone in facing that giant. *"You come at me with sword and spear and javelin,"* he said, *"but I come to you in the name of the Lord. So that all the earth will know the God of Israel, I am going to take you out!"* With God in his heart, a good eye and swift hand, David did just that.

The story is a reminder of several things. The weak can conquer the strong and good can win over evil—but good movies and bedtime stories can tell you that. It is also a reminder that when we who are in the good Lord's army face the giants in our lives, we can defeat them. In short—giants don't have the last word! The world you and I live in does not like that message.

I hate to tell you this, but this is how cable news networks make their money. They capitalize on the Goliaths all around us. One more vote, one more tick down in the stock market, one more act of terrorism— one giant after another. Some churches do the same—telling you about a god who is on your side only if you are on His. God is not "for you," He will really only come to your side if you have got it all together...and not having it all together must mean God's not on your side. It's a vicious circle—and a horrendous cycle—because all of this preys on, and even nourishes our internal fears.

Recently, researchers have figured out where the fear impulse is located in the brain. It's in an area of the brain called the amygdala. One of the most interesting pieces of their research is that external stimuli (say a sound, sight or something that frightens you) travel at breakneck speed from the amygdala to the cerebral cortex—where our thinking about what we see takes place. The connection is pretty much a one-way street, because our reasoning, our making sense out of our fears, is slower. It takes much longer to get back to the fear center to calm it down. Bottom line, it is easy to get the fear center of the brain to tell the reasoning center of the brain what to do, but it is hard to get the reasoning center to say to the source of our fears, "Take it easy, it's going to be okay."

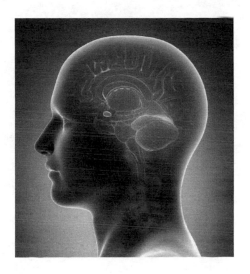

What the world holds up to us when we are facing down those giants—our fears—is a mirror, so that what we see is only ourselves, all alone on the daily battlefields of life. What God wants to hold up for us is a lens that sharpens our eyes, so that when Goliath comes in our view, we know we are not left to our own devices.

David, yes, was armed with a firecracker of a slingshot. Beyond that, he was armed with a confidence that he was not alone—that he had a companion, God Almighty—and that made all the difference in the world.

My mentor, John Claypool, used to like to tell a story about a boy who had been playing ball with a friend in his backyard. A missed catch landed the ball in the yard of a neighbor who had quite the reputation as a bully. When the boy kindly asked for the ball back, the bully refused and took delight in tossing the ball up and down to himself. The boy asked again and the bully only sneered, held up a clinched fist and said, "Come and get it." The boy was shaken for a bit, until he had an idea. He left the yard and went inside, leaving behind an ogre of sorts who thought he had a new ball to add to his collection.

A minute or two later the young boy emerged, but this time with a full-grown man behind him. With a new confidence, he walked right over to the fence, looked the bully in the eyes and said, "I've come to get my ball and I've brung my daddy with me!" The ball was back in his hands in a split second.

I am not trying to make light of what may seem like the giants in your life—life can be hard, at times unbearably hard; but the testimony of Scripture from beginning to end is that God is on our side. The giants do not have the last word—God does! What say you take them on—and bring your Heavenly Daddy with you!

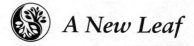 ## A New Leaf

Make a list of the giants in your life right now. Write them down. Take a deep breath or two. You cannot take them on all at the same time, but one by one, consider how you and God can take them on. Remember, He is on your side.

A PRAYER

As the rain hides the stars, as the autumn mist hides the hills, as the clouds veil the blue of the sky, so the dark happenings of my lot hide the shining of Your face from me. Yet, if I may hold Your hand in the darkness, it is enough. Since I know that, though I may stumble in my going, You do not fall.[1] *Amen.*

— Gaelic prayer

1   Translated by Alistair MacLean in *The Doubleday Prayer Collection*, compiled by Mary Batchelor (New York: Doubleday, 1996), p. 166.

You Are the One...

"Then Nathan said to David, 'You are the man!'"

— II Samuel 12:7

Inevitably, there comes a time in the fall when the gutters need to be cleaned out. Leaves, pine straw, tree nuts and grime have filled the gutters—and if it is ignored they just get more clogged. I found this to be a real problem at my own home. I neglected to clean out what seemed to be a rather harmless area of gutter in a corner of my home—not for days, but months...a number of months, to be quite honest. What I did not know is that my negligence had started a small leak that

over those months turned into a large one. Every time we got rain, more water ran behind a wall in our home and finally rotted an entire section of wood, behind sheetrock. You get the picture—it was a mess to clean up, and costly.

I will start this meditation by saying—in my life, I have done a lot of rotten things. I have thought, said and done things that have hurt others, myself and my relationship with God. I know whereof I speak—all too well. Our story calls this kind of behavior "sin," but you may have heard the quip, "Sin is not so much something you do, as something you are in." We all sin. We all do things we wish to God we had not done or fail to do things we wish we had. But you know,

41

to ignore it, deny it, or try and hide it in time means that there's a buildup, and the yuck spills out in all kinds of painful ways—guilt and shame for starters. What to do?

We know David for lots of great things—we also know he did some terrible things. The shepherd who wrote the most quoted of all psalms, Psalm 23, the Old Testament "precursor" to our Lord and Savior Jesus—this same David, we learn, for a season in his life, was also an adulterer and murderer.

The story goes that one day while he was walking around on the roof of his house, he looked down and caught a glimpse of a beautiful young woman named Bathsheba, who was bathing. Immediately his observation turned from lust to covetousness, and he ordered that the woman be brought to him. The two began an intimate affair, and in no time Bathsheba was found with child.

Bathsheba also happened to be married to a Hittite by the name of Uriah. Engulfed with desire, David became obsessed with keeping his ties to Bathsheba. So David befriended Uriah, and ate and drank with him. One night, the partying was so intense, that Uriah basically passed out with intoxication. When he awoke the next morning—no doubt with a tremendous headache—David sent him with a letter to a fellow named Joab.

Now David had a number of battles going on at the time. At that moment, he had just about crushed a group known as the Ammonites. The letter Uriah carried was simple and to the point. The man who believed he had been befriended by Jerusalem's king handed over his own death warrant to Joab. David wrote, *"...Set Uriah in the forefront of the hardest, then draw back from him, so he may be struck down and die."*[1] And that is exactly what happened.

In the days that followed, we find David on a path of self-justification. In fact, he told the messenger who brought him the news, *"Don't let this upset you."* Then, in no time, he lay claim to Bathsheba; had her brought to his home and married her. Then we get this ominous phrase, *"But the thing that David had done displeased the Lord."*[2]

Enter the prophet and advisor to David, Nathan. Nathan put before David a rather long and circuitous metaphor about a rich man stealing a poor man's lamb for his own purposes; and when David became

---

1   II Samuel 11:15.
2   II Samuel 11:27.

infuriated at the image, Nathan lay the gavel down, *"David, you are the man!"* He went on to say, *"You are the man who has despised the word of God, done what is evil, struck down Uriah, taken his wife; killed him..."* In one fell swoop, Nathan pointed out that David had broken no less than four of the Ten Commandments—coveting another man's wife, adultery, deceit and murder.

Bad, bad moment. But what was Nathan's purpose? Was it simply to point the finger and leave it at that? Here was God's appointed and anointed king over Jerusalem—the chosen people of God. Was this the end of the story? *David, bad; story over?* Thank God, no. Nathan's accurate accusation was offering a turning point for David.

As a doctor might point to an X-ray, showing a dark spot on a smoker's lung as the diagnosis for why he has been coughing, Nathan was saying, "David, you need to take a look at what's going on— something is terribly, terribly wrong here." As a physician's diagnosis is usually the beginning point of treatment, so was Nathan's.

What is the takeaway for us here? On the heels of Nathan's diagnosis, a crucial thing happened. When David saw what Nathan was pointing to on that spiritual X-ray of sorts, he was stunned. He said, *"I have sinned against the Lord."* In that moment—that very moment—the admission of guilt, the spiritual clock begins to work backwards and the healing begins. Nathan responded, *"The Lord has put away your sin..."*[3]

Some of us are living with the same kind of conundrum that David faced. Some of us are wrestling with something we know we have done, are doing—some of us need a Nathan to come in and hold up our own spiritual X-ray. In either case, until we come to terms with the sins we have committed, are committing, the healing cannot— will not—begin.

---

3   II Samuel 12:13-14.

It is a very simple principle in psychiatric therapy—the emotionally or mentally troubled patient needs to be able to "name" the core issue that may be bringing about anxiety or distress before the anxiety or distress can begin to go away. The very first step for a recovering alcoholic—the primary step—is admitting there is a problem, an addiction, a darkness which has engulfed his or her life and over which, personally, s/he no longer has control. A key element in understanding the whole saga of God's relationship with us, God's purposes for us, is also learning to allow Him to get the sin out of the way.

Nathan was crystal clear: *"David, what you have done is wrong— w-r-o-n-g...no way around it."* Tough stuff. But then when the light turned on, the good news was shared, *"David, the Lord has put away your sin."* That really is grace, isn't it? Nathan breathed to life one of the key principles in Judeo-Christian faith—humans, by their own merit or work, simply cannot eradicate sin in their own lives, or all the guilt, pain and "yuck" that goes with it. Only God can—but only God can when we bring that to Him.

David had a good many things that one might think would rid him of guilt—power, wealth, prestige—but when he came face-to-face with the truth, all he could do was confess and throw himself into the arms of God's mercy. It did not take away the consequences of his actions, but it did begin to melt the haunting qualities of guilt.

There is more to be said about God's forgiveness, His grace and mercy, and I will touch on that more as we continue our journey, but for now, perhaps, it is time to clean out the gutters. The bad news—you are the one, I am the one who has sinned. The good news? You are the one, I am the one, we are the ones God seeks to forgive, if we would but bring our rubbish to Him. Well?

 # A New Leaf

Want to really turn over a new leaf? Want to rid yourself of that gnawing sense of guilt and shame? Offer your darkness to God... come face to face with the truth, and then hear the good words of Nathan, *"The Lord has put away your sin."*

A PRAYER

Have mercy on me, O God,
according to Your unfailing love;
according to Your great compassion
blot out my transgressions.
Wash away all my iniquity
and cleanse me from my sin...

Create in me a pure heart, O God,
and renew a steadfast spirit within me.[4]
Amen.

---

4 This is drawn from portions of Psalm 51, written by David after Nathan confronted him and assured him of God's mercy.

Choosing Wisely

"At Gibeon the Lord appeared to Solomon in a dream by night; and God said, 'Ask what I should give you.'

"And Solomon said, 'You have shown great and steadfast love to your servant my father David, because he walked before you in faithfulness, in righteousness, and in uprightness of heart toward you; and you have kept for him this great and steadfast love, and have given him a son to sit on his throne today.'

"'And now, O Lord my God, you have made your servant king in place of my father David, although I am only a little child; I do not know how to go out or come in. And your servant is in the midst of people whom you have chosen, a great people, so numerous they cannot be numbered or counted. Give your servant therefore an understanding mind to govern your people, able to discern between good and evil; for who can govern this your great people?'

"It pleased the Lord that Solomon had asked for this."

— I Kings 3:5-10

What is more essential in life—knowledge or wisdom? There is much to be said for knowledge, more for wisdom.

When I was an elementary school student, at the beginning of the school year I really enjoyed going shopping for school supplies—a new ruler, pencils, erasers, a compass and protractor, notebooks, binders—lots of supplies. They would, all of them,

be used. They were tools that got me through the school year for sure, but without wisdom, what good is knowledge?

Sir Isaac Newton was born into an Anglican family. No one would question that he was a brilliant man. He once confessed, "I do not know what I may appear to the world, but to myself I seem to have been only like a boy playing on the seashore, and diverting myself in now and then finding a smoother pebble or a prettier shell than ordinary, whilst the great ocean of truth lay all undiscovered before me." Newton, interestingly, often blended together his vast scientific endeavors and desire to see God's hand, but it was something with which he wrestled most of his life.

Of all Michelangelo's powerful images, one of the most powerful for me is the portrait of the man in *The Last Judgment* being dragged down to hell by demons, one hand over one eye and in the other eye, a look of dire realization. He understood the deeper truths of life, but too late.

The point of our Judeo-Christian story is that there is a "one thing" that God wants to offer us, if we will simply choose wisely. How wonderfully this is told to us in the passage from I Kings! Solomon has now come to his throne as monarch over Israel and Judah, succeeding his father David.

God appears to him in a dream and says, *"Ask what I should give you."*[1] Can you imagine? Talk about hitting the divine jackpot! Solomon replies, *"I am only a little child, and really don't know much...so I guess"*— he says "I guess" above everything— I'll take (not gold, not women, not a huge palace, but) *"an understanding mind to govern your people, able to discern between good and evil."*[2]

The point here is that Solomon knew what mattered most was not something he could get his hands on, or around, but something of infinitely more value—a relationship of ongoing counsel grounded in an unseen God.

Virtually all scientific inquiry is the fruit of the human quest for a deeper truth (see Newton above). There is something very human about searching, about the adventure of a quest. Most people I know are in such a quest almost all the time. But often, what I find, is that

---

1   I Kings 3:5.
2   I Kings 3:6-9; note that sadly, Solomon eventually turned from the wisdom God gave him, and was in time gorging on his fame and wealth, such that in the end there was much sadness in his house.

about the time you reach my age perhaps, if you have spent all of your quest in search of the tangibles, you still feel quite empty; there is still a haunting thirst that is not being quenched.

The Biblical commentator George Arthur Buttrick reflects on this, offering these words,

> Are we not all seekers? Do we not yearn for the farer pearl? Money is good, but not without friendship; friendship is good, but not outside a higher devotion; devotion to art and music is good, but not without a clear conscience; a clear conscience is good, but impossible without forgiveness. So the thoughtful man is ever dissatisfied with moderate joys and shortened goals...Haunting all human eyes is this longing; driving all human steps is this quest...[3]

This quest–this gift, this hunger– is actually a gift from God; but it will eat away at us until we finally feast upon a divine, passionate, reckless, self-abandoning relationship with God.

Essentially, what Solomon wanted was wisdom—not knowledge. He wanted to, in some way, bring the presence of God into the territory known as planet earth. That was a wise choice—it is always a good thing to aim for something other than day-to-day life.

It is a gift of my vocation, but I have spent a lot of time with people in the last moments of their lives—sometimes hearing confessions, sometimes just reflections. I have never heard, "I wish I had earned more...I wish I had bought one more home, a nicer car...I wish I had spent more time at the office...I wish I had had more lovers...or gambled away more money...I wish I had just one more academic degree..." What I have heard and humbly experienced, are lives at their natural end experiencing the fruits of choosing wisely—the Kingdom of God.

C.S. Lewis once wrote, "Aim at heaven and you will get earth thrown in. Aim at earth and you get neither." We are all, all of us, day to day, given Solomon's choice—to live in the counsel of God and His Kingdom, or not. Best to choose wisely.

---

3   George Arthur Buttrick, in "Matthew." Ed. George Arthur Buttrick, The Interpreter's Bible (Nashville: Abingdon, 1979), p. 420. Copyright © 1979 Abingdon Press. Used by permission. All rights reserved.

48

A New Leaf

There is no question there is great value in expanding one's mind, but as Leonard Ravenhill (d. 1994) once wrote "What use is deeper knowledge if we have shallower hearts?" Have you sought more knowledge of this world, or more wisdom about the next? Solomon chose a discerning heart and his choice brought delight to God. Is it a choice you have made?

A PRAYER

God of grace and God of glory,
on thy people pour thy power;
crown thine ancient Church's story;
bring her bud to glorious flower.
Grant us wisdom, grant us courage,
for the facing of this hour.

Lo! the hosts of evil round us
scorn thy Christ, assail his ways!
From the fears that long have bound us
free our hearts to faith and praise:
grant us wisdom, grant us courage
for the living of these days.

Cure thy children's warring madness,
bend our pride to thy control;
shame our wanton, selfish gladness,
rich in things and poor in soul.
Grant us wisdom, grant us courage,
lest we miss thy kingdom's goal.

Save us from weak resignation
to the evils we deplore;
let the gift of thy salvation
be our glory evermore.
Grant us wisdom, grant us courage,
serving thee whom we adore.[4]
Amen.

— Harry Emerson Fosdick, d. 1969

4   In *The Church Hymnal*, #595. Written by Fosdick during the Great Depression.

The Lord—He Is God!

"When all the people saw it, they fell on their faces and said, 'The Lord indeed is God; the Lord indeed is God.'"

— I Kings 18:39

Jesus used not just parables of words to tell stories that revealed deeper truths—but He also, often, used visual aids. In the Sermon on the Mount, Jesus bids His followers to look at the *"lilies of the field... they neither toil nor spin, yet I tell you, even Solomon in all his glory was not clothed like one of these."*[1] It was one way of reminding people not to miss out on seeing God's handiwork in the world around His hearers.

We see a different kind of visual aid in the latter half of I Kings 18, a portion of which is offered above. Here we have a classic clash of the titans. On one side, you have the Canaanites and their prophets of Baal—the god of lightning, storms and fertility. On the other side we have Elijah, God's chosen prophet. Because the people of the northern Kingdom of Israel had been riding the fence between their dedication to Yahweh and the pagan gods of their king, Ahab, Elijah challenged the opposition to a public duel. He even allowed the duel to take place on Mount Carmel—Baal's home turf.

Each side was to build an altar for their god. Elijah, Yaweh's prophet, and the priests of Baal would each cut up a bull for sacrifice and put it on their respective altars. Usually, the practice was then to burn the offering both as a sacrifice of giving up and also to produce a fragrant odor—the kind you might smell at a barbeque cook-off contest. However, in this contest neither Elijah nor the prophets would provide the fire—they would, instead, depend on a fire from heaven. The altar that got fired up first would be the winner and *that* god would then be the god of the people.

---

1   Matthew 6:28–29.

Sure enough, despite a lot of praying, despite the fact that Baal's prophets actually cut themselves with swords and lances to prove their devotion to Baal—they waited, and waited and *nada*—nothing happened. No fire.

It was Elijah's turn. He used 12 stones as a symbol for the 12 tribes of Israel. He dug a trench around the altar. He carefully arranged the pieces of the bull and wood—and as an additional kind of "poke in the eye"—he poured four large jars of water three times over the altar, filling the trench around it with water.

He stood back, and with a kind of "Now watch this" bravado called out to God with the words, *"...let it be known this day that you are God in Israel...Answer me, O Lord, answer me so that this people may know that you, O Lord, are God, and that you have turned their hearts back."*[2]

What happened next? **Fire in the hole!** In a kind of pyrotechnic explosion –the altar, stones, wood, bull and even water were vaporized with a fire that makes a flamethrower look like a cigarette lighter. It was an impressive display that sealed the deal for the people of Israel, who fell on their faces repeating, *"The Lord Indeed is God!"*

Why doesn't God still do that kind of thing? Or does He? Does He, perhaps, all the time?

Writer Annie Farnsworth wrote a thought-provoking fictional piece called "The Angel's Retirement Speech." In it she gives voice to an experienced angel who's addressing some younger colleagues. The elder angel says to the crowd waiting for her wisdom,

> My advice to those of you just starting out: don't expect to make or make too big a splash. They're all so jaded now, what with all this technology. Not like the old days when all you had to do was throw your voice on the wind, cry tears through a statue, maybe just appear in times of great stress, looking your most diaphanous. I guess I would say just stick to the basics, the stuff that always works, like birthing babies, and healing folks the doctors

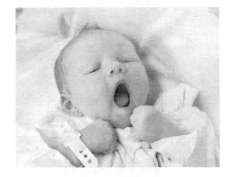

thought hopeless...maybe pull the stalled car off the train tracks at the very last second...when things look grim, give them the old 'Jesus face' in the potato chip, or maybe a squirrel's nest that becomes at dusk...the spitting image of St. Francis in profile.[3]

It's a funny bit, but it makes a point, I think. We can become so distracted that we don't see the miracles around us. We are looking for fire from the sky, when it might be right in front of our eyes.

Do miracles still happen? You'd better believe it. Fall is a great time to see those kinds of miracles—as green leaves gently fade and then are literally transformed to vibrant reds, oranges, yellows. There are scientific explanations for that, of course, but that does not make them any less a miracle. They are happening all the time. Take a look at your hands...look at your fingerprints—the only set like them in all the eons that humans have walked on the face of the earth. That's a miracle right there, would you not agree? But don't keep looking down too long...you will miss so much!

 My old mentor John Stott used to tell the true story of a young man who boasted that once he found a five-dollar bill on the street, he pledged from that time on to never lift his eyes when walking. So in the course of years he accumulated 29,516 buttons, 54,172 pins, 12 cents, a bent back and miserly disposition. But think of what he lost, Stott said. "He couldn't see the radiance of the sunlight, the sheen of the stars, the smile on the face of his friends, or the blossoms of springtime, for his eyes were in the gutter."[4]

Want to witness great miracles? Look up from the distractions —maybe the phone in your hand, the troubles of your heart, the worries of your mind. Look up from your search in the gutter for things that last but a season. Raise your eyes and see the hand of God almost everywhere—raising the sun, setting the moon, speaking through the whimper of the babe in your arms, the look in the eyes of your friend, exactly the moment you needed it most. In all those

3   "The Angel's Retirement Speech" by Annie Farnsworth, from *Bodies of Water, Bodies of Light*. Sheltering Pine Press, 2001.

4   John Stott, "The Biblical Basis for Declaring God's Glory," in *Declare His Glory Among the Nations*, ed. D. M. Howard (Downer's Grove: IVP, 1977), p. 90. CF, *Authentic Christianity*, p. 223.

day-to-day miracles, God is speaking right to you—with the hope that you will lift your eyes from what you are holding to the One who so wants to hold you for all eternity.

Miracles are God's way of saying, *"I am still here—believe in Me, follow Me, know Me, trust me—look on Me—and be transformed."* Indeed, God is still making all things new, still healing souls, and for those who give themselves to Him—He is raising the dead every single day. My guess is—the more you seek, the more you will find; the more you look, the more you will see, and the more you see—the more you will share those ancient words, *"The Lord—He is God!"*

 ## A New Leaf

C.S. Lewis wrote a wickedly fascinating book called *The Screwtape Letters* in which a senior demon, Screwtape, mentors a junior demon, Wormwood, in the ways of tempting humans, whom he calls "patients." In it, he describes one bit of counsel for using the art of distraction this way,

> Keep everything hazy in his mind now, and you will have all eternity wherein to amuse yourself by producing in him the peculiar kind of clarity which Hell affords.[5]

> Indeed, the safest road to Hell is the gradual one—the gentle slope, soft underfoot, without sudden turnings, without milestones, without signposts,... [6]

Toward the end of that counsel, Screwtape warns Wormwood that if God *can break through the distraction,* the patient can become much harder to tempt.

What distractions keep you from seeing the hand of God at work in the world around you? Put it down. Turn it off. Hand it over. Look...seek...find!

---

5 C. S. Lewis, *The Screwtape Letters* (New York: HarperOne, 1996), p. 13.
6 C. S. Lewis, *The Screwtape Letters* (New York: HarperOne, 1996), p. 61.

A Prayer

O Lord, our Lord,
how majestic is Your name in all the earth!
You have set Your glory
above the heavens.
From the lips of children and infants
You have ordained praise...

When I consider Your heavens,
the work of Your fingers,
the moon and the stars,
which You have set in place,
what is man that You are mindful of him,
the son of man that You care for him?...

O Lord, our Lord,
how majestic is Your name in all the earth![6]
Amen.

---

6   This prayer is drawn from Psalm 8.

I Am God...You Are My Child...

"He said, 'Naked I came from my mother's womb, and naked shall I return there; the Lord gave, and the Lord has taken away; blessed be the name of the Lord.'"

— Job 1:21

"...Therefore I have uttered what I did not understand, things too wonderful for me, which I did not know."

— Job 42:3

Though we are not completely sure, it is likely that the common nickname for autumn, "fall," began to be used in the early 1600s. Formerly, the season had been called "harvest," because as summer ended, farmers harvested their crops. As populations became less rural and more urban, those in the cities began to use the word "fall of leaf" to reference the third season when leaves actually begin to "fall." The word *fall* comes from the Old English word *feallan*, which literally translated means "to fall down or to die."

If we think about the word itself, it has far more negative connotations

55

than positive—fallen, fall short, fall down, fall behind, fall away. I could go on, but you get the picture. In the midst of falling, it is hard to think of anything else.

The story of Job is the story of a man whose life literally falls apart. Though it is placed well into the Old Testament, many scholars believe it is one of the oldest stories in the Bible—dating as far back as 2000 B.C. It is a study in *theodicy*, a word theologians use to describe the study of how and why a good God can actually allow suffering in the world. Because of its style, some have suggested it is a parable—inspired truth, rather than literally true. In either case, God has offered it as part of Holy Scripture.[1]

It is a long book, so if you intend to read the whole of it, set aside some time. In the beginning, Job has about all a man could want—family, friends, land, wealth. With God's permission, Satan wages an all-out war on Job—bringing death to Job's family, destruction to his property, even illness to Job's body. In the beginning, Job seems to hold fast to his faith. Over time, three "friends" try and explain to Job that he must have done something wrong because tragedy is falling down all around him. We have all heard the phrase "patience of Job," but soon Job loses his patience…he begins to question why God would allow him as a good man to suffer in such a way. God's response is stark, *"Brace yourself,"* He tells Job. Then God begins a long series of reminders, recalling for Job that God is, well, God; that all that Job's eye can see is born of God's creative power; that there are many things that Job could never fully understand—and, well, suffering as he has suffered is one of them. It is not that God is a divine sadist, nor is it that God is indifferent, but the answer is—God is God.

---

1   For instance, the book opens with a discussion between God and Satan in which Satan proposes a test of tribulations for Job to see if he will remain faithful to God.

That answer will be unsatisfying to anyone seeking a precise answer for those things that befall them in day-to-day life. Some suffering we can understand—a person smokes all his life and gets cancer; a woman eats a high fat diet, never exercises and develops heart disease; someone carelessly leaves a burner on at home and a fire starts. But there are other kinds of suffering that few, if any of us, can ever fully understand—the death of a child, the murder of a loved one, degenerative lingering diseases that appear to have no cure. Is there an answer to these kinds of "falls" in life?

Years ago, I was fortunate to spend an evening with Rabbi Harold Kushner who had written the book, *When Bad Things Happen to Good People*. Of all the wise insights he offered, one thing stood above the rest—"If I wrote a book entitled 'why' bad things happen to good people, it would have been very short —it would simply have been four words, 'I do not know.'" So his reflection on suffering, dealt not so much with *why*, but *when*.[2]

Job's answer to "When bad things happen" is, as hard as it may be to swallow, to still trust. The two scriptures at the beginning of this meditation are really the bookends of Job's full story. The book begins with Job declaring what we all know to be true —we come into this world with nothing and we take nothing from this world. In that, Job finds reason to praise God. At the end of Job's story, even though he has rightly wrestled with his suffering, he realized that the real answer to his questions about his particular suffering is unfathomable, so he turns this fallen season in his own life to one of complete and utter trust in God.

As I read in Rabbi Kushner's book, the author Thornton Wilder wrote a novel entitled, *"The Eighth Day,"* about a good and decent man whose life is ruined by bad luck and hostility. He and his family suffer, although they are innocent. Of course, in many such novels, there is a happy ending; but in this one, there is not. Instead, what Wilder does is offer an image of a beautiful tapestry, which, looked at from the right side is an intricately woven work of art, drawing together threads of different lengths and colors to make up an inspiring picture.

---

2   From Harold Kushner, *When Bad Things Happen to Good People* (New York: Anchor, 1981), pp. 17–18.

If you turn the tapestry over, however, you see a hodgepodge of many threads, some short and some long, some smooth and some cut and knotted, going off in different directions. Wilder offers this as his explanation of how to respond to the reality that good people suffer. God has a pattern into which all of our lives fit. His pattern requires that some lives be twisted and knotted; some cut short while others extend to impressive lengths, not because one thread is more deserving than another, but simply because the pattern requires it. Looked at from underneath, from our vantage point in life, God's pattern of allowing for suffering seems almost arbitrary and without design, like the underside of a tapestry. But looked at from outside this life, from God's vantage point, every twist and knot is seen to have its place in a great design that reveals itself as a work of art.

As a priest, I can tell you that I have sat and prayed with people who have endured unimaginable suffering. There are those who seem to drown in their personal tragedies—and frankly, no one could blame them; I certainly did not. There are those who seem to be treading water at best, and you could not blame them either. But the ones that seem to make it through their valley of troubles without completely collapsing into despair are those who, despite their suffering, and as hard as it may be—continue to trust in God. It did not necessarily assuage all of the pain or suffering—but it did give them a sense of strength to meet the days ahead.

Fall comes...it just comes. Falls come...they just come. If we are looking for an answer, perhaps Job's journey helps point at least one way forward—a reminder of God's assurance—*"I am God, you are my child."* Sometimes that can be enough.

A New Leaf

How have you suffered? Are you suffering? If you have been searching for a reason for your suffering with the word *why*, perhaps shift your perspective by using the word *when*. How could the word *trust* be a comfort to you in your suffering?

A Prayer

Almighty and Heavenly Father, be present with me in my sufferings.
If there is no reason for me to grasp, then let me hold fast to You.
If there is no relief for my pain, then revive me with Your grace.
If there is no end in sight, let me place my eyes on You.
If the time of tribulation is brief, give me a grateful heart for its end;
      if it is long, then give me courage and strength to face the
      days ahead.

In all things, let my faith and trust in You never falter;
      and when life is falling down around me;
      give me humility to fall before You,
      and in doing so to find in Your presence,
      Your abiding peace.

In the name of Your Son, Jesus Christ, who suffered for the sake and salvation of all.
Amen.

Heaven's Gate

"Give ear to my words, O Lord;
give heed to my sighing.
Listen to the sound of my cry,
my King and my God,
for to you I pray.
O Lord, in the morning you hear
my voice;
in the morning I plead my case
to you, and watch."

— Psalm 5:1–3

This is a beautiful passage. The Book of Psalms includes 150 prayers—long, short and everything in between—likely crafted over hundreds of years from around 1400 to 500 B.C. A variety of authors crafted the prayers—David, Solomon, Moses—but many do not mention an author. Prayer is frankly time set aside to be with God—to be still before God, praise Him, thank Him, confess to Him, ask Him, plead to Him. Prayer can be a song, word spoken, laughter, weeping, expressed anger, overwhelming joy. Prayer can be about anything one places before God in God's presence.

I wrote a bit earlier that often when fall comes, there are things we do to prepare for the season. Perhaps we put away our summer clothes and pull out sweaters, hats and gloves. If you are a homeowner, you may have your heating units inspected or your fireplace cleaned. Maybe you put away hoses and garden tools. You "prepare" for the season to come. Praying is a way of preparing, but not for a season—for all of life and life yet to come.

My mentor John Stott once wrote, "The reason why Christian people are drawn to the psalms is that they speak the universal language of the human soul," and then, quoting British author Rowland E. Prothero, he affirmed that the psalms "contain the whole music of the heart of man."[1] Such are the psalms—such is prayer.

Richard Foster, a Quaker, in his wonderful book, *Celebration of Discipline,* reminds his reader that "Prayer catapults us onto the frontier of the spiritual life. Of all the Spiritual Disciplines prayer is the most central because it ushers us into perpetual communion with the Father."[2]

The Bible is full of prayers. There are untold volumes written on the "how to" and "when to" pray. These are helpful, but in the end it is not so much about *how you pray,* but *that* you pray.

Break for just a moment—in a moment of silence, if you had something to offer to God, ask of God, tell God right now, what would it be? Go ahead... do it now...I will wait...

Did you tell Him what was on your mind? In your heart? That was prayer! There is more to it than that, but that is essentially what prayer is.

When Jesus talked to His followers about prayer, He did not presume they would not pray—in fact, His assumption was that they would! As He began to teach them what you and I know as "The Lord's Prayer," He said, *"And when you pray...."*[3] Not "if," but "when."

Prayer really is a gift. We have a God who is interested in us personally. He wants to spend time with us and wants us to spend time with

---

1   John Stott, *Favorite Psalms* (Grand Rapids: Baker Books, 1988), p. 5.
2   Richard Foster, *Celebration of Discipline* (San Francisco: Harper & Row, 1988), p. 33.
3   Matthew 6:5ff.

Him. Reading the Psalms, praying with them, is one way to spend that time, and really, any time like that—any time we are in prayer—we are merely drawing closer to the One with whom we will spend eternity—we are drawing closer to heaven itself.

There is a beautiful line from a poem by William Blake (d. 1827) entitled, "Jerusalem: The Emanation of the Giant Albion." It reads simply,

> I give you the end of a golden string
> Only wind it into a ball
> It will lead you in at Heavens gate
> Built in Jerusalems wall[4]

As you prepare for the autumn season, may you find prayer to be a gift that prepares you for the life abundant here, and the life yet to come.

 ## A New Leaf

If you are reading this book, you are likely already one who practices the gift of prayer. If so, give thanks that you can have an ongoing conversation with God Almighty—creator of heaven and earth!
If not, or if it is something you do when everything else is done, consider praying through the Psalms—start a portion of a psalm or one each day, through the days to come. Pray with them, let them pray through you—know you are winding a golden string that will lead you in at Heaven's gate.

---

4   William Blake, "Jerusalem: The Emanation of the Giant Albion," in *The Poetry and Prose of William Blake*, ed. David V. Erdman (Garden City, New York: Doubleday & Company, 1965), p. 229.

A PRAYER

Praise the Lord.
Praise God in his sanctuary;
>   praise him in his mighty heavens.
Praise him for his acts of power;
>   praise him for his surpassing greatness.
Praise him with the sounding of the trumpet,
>   praise him with the harp and lyre,
praise him with tambourine and dancing,
>   praise him with the strings and flute,
praise him with the clash of cymbals,
>   praise him with resounding cymbals.
Let everything that has breath praise the Lord.
Praise the Lord.
Amen.

>   — Psalm 150

Do You Really Want to Grow?

"Cease straying, my child, from the words of knowledge, in order that you may hear instruction."

— Proverbs 19:27

Since my youth, I have always enjoyed camping. While I've camped in each season of the year, my favorite time is fall—not too hot, not too cold, just cool enough. While I learned a great deal from my parents about many things in life, camping was not one of them—we were not a camping family.

I learned some things from summer camps I attended, but I suppose most of what I learned, at least in my first several camp outs, was from my next door neighbor, David, who was a devoted Boy Scout. I was not a Scout, but was a friend to David, and he to me. From what he had learned, I learned how to build a fire, make a temporary hammock or clothesline, and make a stove out of a coffee can! Key to my learning was a willingness to learn.

There are a great many wise words offered in proverbial style. *Meditations* by Marcus Aurelius (d. 180 A.D.) and *The Prophet* by Kahlil Gibran (d. 1931) come to mind, but these are not considered sacred texts, whereas the Book of Proverbs is. Most of the proverbs were written by Solomon, so the words were collected sometime during his reign (around 970 to 930 B.C.).

Much like the Psalms, reading through the Proverbs a bit at a time would be a worthy task. Though written some 3,000 years ago, the insights offered through Proverbs can apply as easily today as they did in their own day...

> *"Trust in the Lord with all your heart,*
> *and do not rely on your own insight.*
> *In all your ways acknowledge him,*
> *and he will make straight your paths."*
>
> 3:5–6

> *"A gossip goes about telling secrets,*
> *but one who is trustworthy in*
> *spirit keeps a confidence."*
>
> 11:13

> *"In the path of righteousness there is life,*
> *in walking its path there is no death."*
>
> 12:28

> *"Pride goes before destruction,*
> *a haughty spirit before a fall."*
>
> 16:18

Hover on that last one a moment. As I now look down the road toward the age of 60, one of the things I have found in our time is that many young adults have abandoned what was, to me, one of the most helpful of all my life's experiences—having mentors. I have been fortunate to have a number of them. My father and mother were mentors for

sure. My wife and children have been mentors. There have also been wise, experienced men and women—most of whom I sought out—who have helped me see life in different ways. The way I learned, frankly, was to sit at their feet, ask questions, listen and allow their experience to speak to my own. I suppose I could have at some point said, "I have learned about all I need to know, I'll take it from here" (see "pride" above!). But it would have been to my great loss.

One of the most important mentors in my life, someone I have already referenced in this book, was the late John Claypool, an Episcopal priest, under whom I served for six years, but with whom

I had a very close relationship for more than two decades until his death. I still remember a very powerful sermon he preached that had quite an impact on me, entitled, "Do You Really Want to Grow?" It was focused on the text of Mark 1:1–8, which told the story of John the Baptist's ministry of calling others to "repent." But John used the text as an opportunity to encourage his hearers to consider their willingness to change. For instance, he said, in his experience the most important single ingredient in a successful marriage is the desire to make it work. He went on to say if that reality was present in both parties, there is hardly any conceivable difficulty that they cannot find a way to overcome. However, if such a desire is not present, no amount of favorable circumstances can guarantee the success of the marriage. That is true in almost all of our relationships—is it not? And it is certainly true about personal growth. If we are willing to learn, there will be plenty yet to do; if we are willing to grow, we will grow until our last breath on earth.

To go back to where I began, to this day I am indebted to my friend David. To this day, and every day yet to come, I am in debt to my mentors. If you are willing to grow, pick up the Book of Proverbs and let them show you yet another way.

 A New Leaf

The wisest people I know are those still willing to learn. I would bet the same is true for you. To whom could you turn today to get a new understanding of life? I suggest you make that turn—today.

A Prayer

Blessed Lord, which hast caused all holy Scriptures to be written for our learning; grant us that we may in such wise hear them, read, mark, learn, and inwardly digest them; that by patience and comfort of thy holy word, we may embrace, and ever hold fast the blessed hope of everlasting life, which thou hast given us in our saviour Jesus Christ. *Amen.*

— Thomas Cranmer, d. 1556

To Whom Should You Go?

"The word of the Lord came to Jonah a second time, saying, 'Get up, go to Nineveh, that great city, and proclaim to it the message that I tell you.'"

— Jonah 3:1–2

Over the years, I have lived in more than a dozen different homes—some I rented, others the bank and I owned together. Some had fireplaces; others did not. There are few things more enjoyable than a crackling fire invited by the cool breezes of autumn. When I was a younger man, there were times I had to split firewood. I remember

the first time I did split wood, I assumed it was easy—having seen the likes of Davy Crockett episodes on television when all he did was raise a hatchet and crack a log in two with a quick whack. I was completely wrong. To split more than a few pieces of wood would rival an aerobics class of any length of time.

If you have ever done it you know there are five things required: a "wedge" of metal you tap into the wood; sledge hammer to deepen the work of the wedge; hatchet or axe to finish the physical work; willingness to do the work; and perhaps most importantly, doing the work! You could have every tool in the world and every good intention in the world, but unless you put them all to use, the wood is not going to get split—the fire is not going to burn.

Have you ever read the book of Jonah? If you hear "Jonah," what is the first thing that comes to mind? Most likely it is "whale"! Many a Vacation Bible School program has been built around the story of Jonah and the whale, but we have edited the story a good bit when we pass it on to our young ones. Jonah is not a book about a whale. In fact, there is no mention of a whale at all—it is a "great fish," and it is only mentioned three times!

Jonah is written in the third person, so we do not know who its author was. We do find him mentioned in II Kings as one who prophesied during the reign of Israel's King Jeroboam II, who was king from about 793 to 753 B.C.[1] Because of its style, as was suggested about the Book of Job, it is possible it is an inspired story. Again, whether literal or story, it is still true and still has a deep truth to offer, and the truth is about God's love for unlovable people.

In sum, God calls on Jonah to preach to the people of Nineveh, the capital of the brutal Assyrian Empire. Jonah had no interest in guiding those he considered to be godless people to a loving God. He not only disobeys God, but also runs from the task. That is where the great fish comes in—nothing like spending three days in the belly of a whale (or giant grouper if you will) to change your mind about doing something God is calling you to do.

Jonah repents (while in the belly of that fish). God sends a bit of divine ipecac to Mr. Whale, who in turn, *spewed Jonah out upon the dry land*—right onto the shore of Nineveh.[2] God tells Jonah, once again (hence the phrase "a second time" in the meditation verse) to preach. Jonah preaches, the entire nation turns to God, and in the end, Jonah is still ticked that God would waste His time. God's response to Jonah's pout is, *"And should I not be concerned about Nineveh, that great city…?"*[3] Jonah's response is left unrecorded—that is not the version we usually tell in Vacation Bible School.

The Book of Jonah (the whole of which you could read in about half an hour or less) is about reconciliation—about God's love for unlovable and unloving people—a theme which will dominate the second half of this book. Jonah was supposed to light a fire under the Ninevites—God gave Him all the tools necessary to get the job done, but in the end, if he did not do what he had been called to do, the

---

1   Cf., II Kings 14:23–25.
2   Jonah 2:10.
3   Jonah 4:11.

reconciliation between God and a rebellious people would not have occurred.

Harder than splitting wood—infinitely harder—is the work of reconciliation. An entire book could be written (and many have been written) on reconciliation itself. But one could read all the books available, have all the circumstances in place, and yet—if the active process of reconciliation does not begin—reconciliation will not occur.

To get down to brass tacks, is there someone with whom you should reconcile today? The Scriptures are filled with counsel on the importance of God's children seeking forgiveness when they have hurt another, shedding mercy when asked, and loving one another, despite past hurts or wounds. Now, it should be noted, that it is true—some parties will be unwilling to reconcile. Even Jesus had clear words about beating your head against an unwilling party, *"If anyone*

will not welcome you or listen to your words, shake off the dust from your feet as you leave that house or town."[4] Nevertheless, when possible, we are to seek reconciliation with others, between others, any time we can. We are, in a sense, as God's children to be ambassadors of reconciliation.[5]

Archbishop Desmond Tutu, who has spent a lifetime preaching and modeling authentic reconciliation, reminds us that such work is hard but is also a reflection of the compassion of God Himself. He wrote, "Some people think reconciliation is a soft option, that it means papering over the cracks. But the biblical meaning means looking facts in the face and it can be very costly; it cost God the death of His own Son." Again, it is hard work.

But you know, it is work we are called to do—work God calls us to do. Even, as Jonah shows us, if we do not want to do it, we are still called to give it a try. Why? Because God cares for and loves everyone—and the most effective way we can share that good news is to, as much as humanly possible, care for and love others.

Jonah was sent to the Ninevites. To whom should you go?

---

4   Matthew 10:14.
5   See II Corinthians 5:11–21.

A New Leaf

A pause in your reading will likely bring to mind, right away, someone with whom you may need to reconcile. If not that, perhaps someone who needs to know that God loves them and seeks to be reconciled with them. You have all the tools to do this—can you put them to work? Pick up the phone, write the letter, make the visit—let reconciliation begin, today.

A Prayer

Lord of the loving heart, may mine be loving too,
Lord of the gentle hands, may mine be gentle too.
Lord of the willing feet, may mine be willing too,
So may I grow more like you
In all I say or do.[6]
Amen.

— From "All Our Days"

---

6   *The Doubleday Prayer Collection*, compiled by Mary Batchelor (New York: Doubleday, 1996), p. 58.

Trusting in the Unseen

"Though the fig tree does not blossom,
and no fruit is on the vines;
though the produce of the
olive fails and the field yield no food;
though the flock is cut off from the fold,
and there is no herd in the stalls,
yet I will rejoice in the Lord;
I will exult in the God of my salvation."

— Habakkuk 3:17–18

I am no botanist, but let me give this a try. This time of year, why do our leaves change color from green, to vibrant color, and then fall to the ground as if dead? As summer winds down and the days get shorter, trees begin to prepare for the winter because the longer days of summer, which allow for more light and the process of photosynthesis, begin to wane. Trees, literally, begin to rest—they cut back on their food-making processes. The green chlorophyll is "drained" from the leaves as the trees begin to live off the food they have stored during the summer months.

As the green goes away, we see vibrant colors of red, yellow, orange, purple and so on, but those colors were really there all along. They were simply not visible because the green chlorophyll dominated. Eventually, as the nourishment of the leaves completely withdraws, they dry up and fall to the ground. Fortunately, we also know that is not the end of the trees' lives—just a season.

It is not a leap to my next point; much of the latter part of the Old Testament is made up of books of the prophets—there are what biblical scholars call Major Prophets (think Isaiah, Jeremiah, Ezekiel) and Minor Prophets (think Obadiah, Micah, Nahum). Essentially the work of the prophets had three parts— to tell God's people (or the nations) when they had turned from God, to call them to return back to God, and when they did  not, and all seemed lost, to remind them that despite all appearances there was still reason to rejoice. Such is the case with the brief passage above from Habakkuk.

The nation of Israel divided into two kingdoms because of (a vast understatement here) leadership. Over time, both nations and their leaders turned from God. Prophets came with warning after warning that turning from God also meant impending doom. Other godless nations would defeat and destroy what had taken so long to build up—and indeed those prophecies came to pass. The northern Kingdom of Israel fell to the Assyrians in 722 B.C., and the southern Kingdom of Judah fell to the Babylonians in 587 B.C. All seemed lost. Habakkuk describes the desolation throughout his own contribution to the Scriptures in three short chapters.

Yet nestled into all the bad news there is some good—in fact, it is so good, it becomes a pillar throughout the rest of the Judeo-Christian story, *"the righteous live by their faith."*[1] Recall the meditation on Abram, in which Abram *"believed"* and God credited it to him as righteousness.[2] Here, as we come to the close of the Old Testament, we get yet another whisper that faith is really the bedrock of a relationship with God. It is not so much what one experiences or sees, but more what he or she believes, even when all evidence to the contrary may prevail.

---

1   Habakkuk 2:4.
2   Genesis 15:6.

Habakkuk reminds the southern Kingdom of Judah that though everything they knew to be good about their lives and nation was being wiped away before their very eyes—they should still rejoice in the Lord and still trust in God. They could not live by what they saw—if they did, they would be utterly devastated. Instead they lived by faith.

If an alien were plopped onto planet Earth as autumn's final days came to an end, it would have absolutely no idea that what appeared to be dried up, dead or dying brown trees would one day again be covered with full, green leaves—literally breathing oxygen into our world.

God uses His prophets to teach people to always trust in God. When things seem at their worst, God still writes the final chapter. It is something we see time and time again throughout all of Scripture—with its consummate moment being Jesus' resurrection. On Good Friday no one, not even the apostles, expected Easter Sunday. Love divine had been crucified and love divine rose from the grave.

What desolation are you facing this day? What death rests before you? Does all seem lost? There is a way ahead—trust, trust in the unseen. Trust in God. The righteous person shall live by his faith.

 ## A New Leaf

Thomas Merton once wrote, "Ultimately, faith is the only key to the universe. The final meaning of human existence, and the answer to the questions on which all our happiness depends cannot be found in any other way." It is a beautiful passage, but we can, at times, find faith—that trust in the unseen—to be a hard beginning place. You are not alone. Remember when a father came to Jesus and asked Him to heal his son? Jesus said to him, "If you are able!—All things can be done for the one who believes." Immediately the father of the child cried out, "I believe; help my unbelief!"[3]

Perhaps if you need more faith, you just need to ask for it. Martin Luther wrote, "Believing in God means getting down on your knees." Well?

---

3   Mark 9:23–24.

A PRAYER

While faith is with me, I am blest;
It turns my darkest night to day;
But while I clasp it to my breast,
I often feel it slide away.

Then, cold and dark my spirit sinks,
To see my light of life depart;
And every friend of Hell, methinks,
Enjoy the anguish of my heart.

What shall I do, if all my love,
My hopes, my toil, are cast away,
And if there be no God above,
To hear and bless me when I pray?

Oh, help me, God! For Thou Alone
Canst my distracted soul relieve.
Forsake it not: it is Thine own,
Though weak, yet longing to believe...

...I need not fear my foes;
I need not yield to care;
I need not sink beneath my woes,
For Thou wilt answer prayer.

In my Redeemer's name,
I give myself to Thee;
And, all unworthy as I am,
My God will cherish me. *Amen.*

— Anne Brontë, d. 1849

74

There's More to the Story

"See, I am sending my messenger to prepare the way before me…"

— Malachi 3:1

"…Return to me, and I will return to you, says the Lord of hosts."

— Malachi 3:7

As I wrote back in the introduction, this devotional is divided between the Old Testament and the New. I am not suggesting the 20 meditations on pieces of the Hebrew scriptures in any way plumbs the depths of the treasure that rests in its 39 books. The intent has been more like taking a rock and skimming it across the surface of the water—but with each skip, hopefully there has been some helpful thought and perhaps you have stopped along the way to dive a bit deeper.

But for now, we have come to the end of the Old Testament— Malachi. We know nothing of him, other than his name. Literally translated it means "my messenger." The book was probably written around 450 B.C. Sadly, as we come to this close, the message is similar to much of what the prophets of old shared—God's people have begun to take their relationship with God for granted, they have neglected their call to worship God and to serve Him. Through Malachi, God tells His children that the sacrifices they bring are *"blind"* and *"sick"* (1:8);

the men divorce their godly wives to marry pagan women (2:11, 14); and that they have begun to *"rob God"* by not supporting His temple with tithes and offerings (3:6–9).

The book ends with a stark warning that if the Lord is not honored and the people do not return to Him, then He promises He *"will come and strike the land with a curse"* (4:6). If this was God's last word to His children, things would certainly look bleak. From what we know, there are no further books of holy text offered for nearly 400 years. But like almost every book of Scripture, there are—nestled within the layers of bad news—promises of good news.

One is offered in Malachi 3:1. It is a foreshadowing of the coming of John the Baptist who would, in fact, prepare the way of the Lord. When Mark (our earliest Gospel) describes John the Baptist, he draws on this very verse.[1] There is offered here a preview of coming attractions. What appears to be the end of the story is not; and beneath that promise of a messenger coming, we have God's hand held out yet again—*"return to me, and I will return to you."* God, it seems, never stops trying to reach out to us.

If you have taken this on as intended, an autumn devotional, by now the leaves are likely gone from the trees; the bright and long sunny days have become darker and shorter. From all appearances things look rather bleak, and through that lens alone, it would appear that the future holds little promise.

But what do you and I know? We know that after fall, after winter—spring comes. There is not just the hope of another season—there is the certainty of it. The end of things is not the end.

I once heard a poet wonderfully describe what rests behind a crescent moon. He said when the moon is waxing from crescent to full, all we can see from earth is a small sliver—but that does not mean the whole moon is not there—it is, and over time it will be revealed in its fullness.

---

1   Mark 1:2; cf. Isaiah 40:3.

Such is the story of God's ongoing relationship with us. If Malachi's last words to us were a curse—we would be left with only a sliver of God's revelation, but there is more to come—much more! The fullness of God's love will be revealed. Sit tight—there's more to the story.

 A New Leaf

In a sense, Malachi invites us to hope. Mixed in among the true assessment of God's children are reminders of God's hope that His children will return to Him. That hope should inspire hope within us as well—hope that even when things seem quite dark, when God seems very distant, that does not have to be the last word. Thomas Benton Brooks, a Puritan pastor and author, wrote, "Hope can see heaven through the thickest clouds." What clouds are fogging up your view of heaven today? Ask God for hope—He will deliver.

A PRAYER

Lord, if you will make
the autumn of my life
as lovely as this golden autumn morning,
I will not look back to grieve the passing days of summer.
Of all the regal seasons autumn is the most brilliant.
Make my life brilliant, too!
Amen.

— Ruth Harms Calkin

Half-Time

*"...because we look not at what can be seen but
at what cannot be seen; for what can be seen is
temporary, but what cannot be seen is eternal."*

— II Corinthians 4:18

Let me invite you to pause for a moment between the first part of this offering of scriptures, mediations and prayers and the second part. The Bible, Holy Scripture, is a story; but for Christians it is more than any story. It is a true story, an inspired story, a love story—a story of God's love for His children.

Are we that lovable? As I type these words, I reflect on my read of the morning paper. I did not have to look far before horrible stories of crime and violence were before my very eyes. I can think on the lives of those who have hurt me. I do not have to sit long with sincerity of heart before I know there are those things I have done and left undone. Let us be honest, there seems to be less to love rather than more, and yet— God persistently pursues us.

Some school children may have had to read or memorize the well-known and crafted poem "The Hound of Heaven," by Francis Thompson (d. 1907). The opening stanza unveils a story familiar to many of us.

> I fled Him, down the nights and down the days;
>   I fled Him, down the arches of the years;
> I fled Him, down the labyrinthine ways

Of my own mind; and in the mist of tears
I hid from Him, and under running laughter.
   Up vistaed hopes I sped;
   And shot, precipitated,
Adown Titanic glooms of chasmèd fears,
  From those strong Feet that followed, followed after.
   But with unhurrying chase,
   And unperturbèd pace,
Deliberate speed, majestic instancy,
   They beat—and a Voice beat
   More instant than the Feet—
'All things betray thee, who betrayest Me.'

The poem, of course, is about the persistent pursuit of God. There are times when we might feel our sins, our life, who we are—essentially, is beyond God's reach, beyond His redemption. But if that is the case, why then do we find throughout the Old Testament a God of not just second chances, but of yet agains?

Let that last line hang just a moment—*"All things betray thee, who betrayest Me."* God does not, it seems, cease to remind us that as long as we make choices, or turn directions, away from Him that we are actually choosing things that betray Him—and more so, making choices that rob us of the things we all want—abundant life, forgiveness, joy, peace salvation.

When my daughter was a child, one of her favorite animated Disney films was *Beauty and the Beast*. She could watch it over and over again. The core message of the movie is something we all need to hear—that a beast can in fact be transformed by love.

We are now going to turn to the New Testament, which, of course reveals the greatest manifestation of love; but it is no fairy tale love and it is no love born of a human's will—it is divine love, transcendent love, sacrificial love, redemptive love—a love beyond all loves.

In many worship services there is a moment called "the Peace." In my tradition, it falls about mid-way through the service, at half-time we might say. The first half of the service has been filled with introductory prayers, scriptures, perhaps a hymn or two, a sermon, one of the ancient creeds, the prayers and confession. The "design" if you will of the liturgy in this way is to intentionally prepare one for the second part of the service—Holy Communion—a sacramental

79

moment of connection with Jesus Christ and all the saints of God that have been, are and are yet to be.

"The Peace" was an ancient practice in the Church that actually finds its roots in Paul's letter to the Romans when he enjoins Christians to *"Greet one another with a holy kiss."*[1] While its placement in worship 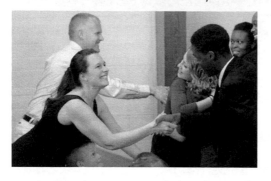 has shifted over the years, most believe it has found its rightful place in the middle of the worship service. The first half of the service was designed to move the worshiper from the world into the scriptures, preaching of the Word, prayer and confession. Then, having been offered by God an invitation to confess where the penitent has fallen short, the worshiper—now reminded of God's forgiveness in the redemptive work of Jesus Christ—may be sure to approach Jesus' table at peace with God, with him or herself, and with others. If he or she does not feel "at peace," then, in fact there is a need for more reflection—is there something yet unconfessed? Is the worshiper living in enmity with someone? Does the worshiper have unresolved feelings or thoughts toward God? Whatever the case, "the peace" provides a moment to do our part in responding to God's grace and love toward us.

I hope this "half-time" moment gives you an opportunity to reflect on anything you have gained from these pages thus far. Is there something that you may need to confess to our Lord? Is there some area that needs pruning? Is there reconciling work to be done? Or, might you need to simply rest in the reminders of His love for you? His desire to make you whole? To forgive you? Comfort you? Save you?

Before we move on—may His peace be yours, and as we continue, may that peace be a companion on our journey to come.

---

1   Romans 16:16; cf. I Corinthians 16:20, II Corinthians 13:12; I Thessalonians 5:26 and I Peter 5:14.

A PRAYER

Let us not seek out of Thee what we can only find in Thee, O Lord: peace and rest and joy and bliss, which abide only in Thine abiding joy.

Lift up our souls above the weary round of harassing thoughts to Thy eternal presence.

Lift up our minds to the pure, bright serene atmosphere of Thy presence, that we may breathe freely, there repose in Thy love, there be at rest from ourselves and from all things that weary us; and thence return, arrayed in Thy peace, to do and to bear whatsoever shall best please Thee, O blessed Lord. *Amen.*

— The Reverend Canon Edward Bouverie Pusey, d. 1882

Salt and Light

"You are the salt of the earth…"

"You are the light of the world…"

— Matthew 5:13, 14

....

The Sermon on the Mount, which we find in Matthew's Gospel as well as Luke's, comes together as some of the most beautiful of all words ever spoken.[1] A.B. Bruce wrote of the Sermon on the Mount, *"we are near heaven."*[2]

I was fortunate, some time ago, to visit the Church of the Beatitudes, found on a hilltop overlooking the Sea of Galilee. The day I was there, the sun was shining, there was a gentle wind and the water from Galilee was so calm the waves were gently lapping upon its shores. I tried to imagine (as I suspect every visitor does) that day when Jesus was speaking to His followers. By then, already, His reputation as a teacher and healer had spread, the crowds were growing, people were following. Jesus had them sit down, Matthew records, and then He began that wonderful reflection on what it means to live a godly life; and what those who wish to follow Him should do.

Matthew's Gospel (Gospel meaning "good news") was probably written around 70 A.D. and he tells his own story in chapter nine. It records Jesus' life, ministry, death and resurrection from the unique perspective of a Jew who sees in Jesus the fulfillment of the Old Testament prophecies.

Matthew's given name was evidently Levi, as Mark notes in his Gospel.[3] The Levites were those Hebrews commissioned by God through Moses to be the priests who served the Temple of God and

---

1   Luke 6:20–23.
2   A.B. Bruce died in 1899. Note the full text of the Sermon on the Mount includes Matthew 5:1–7:29.
3   Mark 2:14.

who, upon the Exodus, were given the unique responsibility of carrying the Ark of the Covenant.[4]

The point of this background is that Matthew, as he described himself, was by this time a tax collector; frowned upon by the average Jew in Jesus' day, Matthew was thus a bit of a turncoat. A descendant of the Levites, he had taken on the duty of collecting taxes for the state—no priest—rather, he was a public servant squeezing funds to serve the state's purposes.

When Jesus called to Matthew, *"Follow me,"* we are told he got up from the tax collector's table, left his work and life behind, and followed. Only hours later he hosted a dinner party of other tax collectors and, in his own words, sinners. When the religionists called Jesus out for associating with this type of folk, He quickly responded, *"Those who are well have no need of a physician, but those who are sick."*[5]

To circle back to the Sermon on the Mount, Jesus said a lot of things, but one striking thing is that He told His hearers it is not God alone who brings good things to the world, but His followers as well. Can you imagine how Matthew must have felt to have gone from an outcast of society, and the people of his faith, to taking in Jesus' words, *"You are the salt of the earth…the light of the world"*? Why would it mean so much to Matthew?

Every home in ancient Israel, no matter how poor, used salt and light. During His own childhood, Jesus probably watched his mother Mary use salt in the kitchen and light oil lamps when the sun would go down. Salt and light were two indispensable household commodities.

Salt had a wide variety of purposes, but chiefly it was a condiment to add flavor to food and also a preservative to keep food from decay. Light provided a way to work, study and be in community when darkness enshrouded the day.

Jesus was saying, on one hand there is "the earth," and on the other hand there is "you" who

---

4   Read more about their duties in Numbers 18.
5   See Matthew 9:9–13.

are the earth's salt. On one hand there is "the world," and on the other hand there is "you" who are the world's light. What this means, of course, is an incredible acknowledgment of the life of Matthew. In the midst of a dark and crumbling world, this one who was shunned by many was being recognized by Jesus as that same world's salt and light.

Matthew would have heard the words to mean "you are the salt" and so you are to add flavor to the world around you and preserve it from decay. "You are the light" and so you are to shine what you know of God's love, mercy and grace to the world around you. What Jesus was saying, quite frankly, was He believed that His followers could make a difference—He believed that Matthew could make a difference. If these are words to Jesus' followers, then this also is a word to you!

I wonder if you believe you can really make a difference in the world?

When fall comes, the days are shorter, the world is colder. Darkness and cold are good metaphors for what many of us find when we read the daily news—does our world not seem that it may be in need of the kind of salt and light Jesus suggested should be sprinkled in the lives of His followers?

We, of course, do this in all kinds of ways—the way we live in our private lives (our thoughts, motives, intentions, prayers) and public lives (the way we interact with others, through our work, play, habits), and how we deal with our fault lines (when we fail to live as we should, bringing our failings to the mercy of God, receiving His grace, our commitment to returning again and again to His arms and transforming power). But in the end, in a sense, it is simply about "believing" we are called to be salt and light—even if others think we are not so, even if we doubt our own abilities. There is Jesus, on that mount, reminding us to persist, to not give in to the belief that we cannot, you cannot, in some way impact the darkness and decay of the world.

I have a friend who tells me he believes there are basically two kinds of people, "putter-inners" and "taker-outers." What he means, of course, is that there are those people who, no matter what life hands them, seem to be able to make the most out of it. While they are not naïve about the trials of life, they are also not morose and hung up on them.

Then, on the other hand, there are those people who always see the glass as half empty. They can look at a completely white sheet and immediately focus on the small dark spot. They are the kind of people that even if they were put in the Garden of Eden, they would find something to criticize.

To the taker-outer, Jesus says, *"You have the opportunity to turn that around—you have the opportunity to take what may seem dark and sinister and dying and pour life into it. Follow me, and I'll help you do precisely that."* To the putter-inner, Jesus affirms what you already know, *"You are the salt of the earth...you are the light of the world. Well done! Keep at it...you and I are in this together. Get to sprinkling, get to shining—the world needs it."*

 A New Leaf

Do you believe Jesus' words? Do you see yourself as salt and light? Are you a "putter-inner" or a "taker-outer?" Augustus W. Hare, a German historian who died in 1834, once reflected, "In darkness there is no choice. It is light than enables us to see the difference between things; and it is Christ that gives us light." If you find yourself struggling to be salt and light, ask Christ for it—ask for it now—that you may be as He has called on you to be.

A Prayer

Lord Jesus, my Lord Jesus,
some days, I see only the darkness,
  some days there seems to be no light at all.
The decay of a damp and dying world, at times, I must confess,
  simply overwhelms my senses, weighs so heavy on my heart,
  draws life from my soul.

How can I be light when I can see no light?
How can I be salt, when all I see is decay?

Only through You,
  only by You, only with You, only...
  You.

Forgive me Jesus for denying Your power to transform me.
Release me from the bondage of a world seen only through my eyes.
Renew me that I may, by Your grace and mercy, be the child of God
You created me to be, You call me to me, You need me to be.

Help me Jesus, help me to be salt, to be light,
for Your sake and the sake of the world.
Amen.

Get Some Rest

*"The apostles gathered around Jesus, and told him
all that they had done and taught. He said to them,
'Come away to a deserted place all by yourselves
and rest a while.' For many were coming and going,
and they had no leisure even to eat. And they went
away in the boat to a deserted place by themselves."*

— Mark 6:30–32

When you read this passage, what do you feel? Does part of you—right now—go, "That would be nice…a quiet place…a solitary place…by myself…to get some rest." Honestly, it certainly speaks to me in that way.

As noted before, seasonal changes often bring new duties. Because the days are shorter in autumn, one often has to cram more things into the day's hours to get what seems to be important done. But no one—no one—is meant to run the engines of life beyond their capacity to function with a sense of normalcy. Most of the ailments we humans suffer upon ourselves are the fruit of wearing out life's gears: physical (heart disease, stroke, many cancers, addictions); emotional and mental (some forms of depression and compulsion, anxiety, angst, stress, worry); and certainly spiritual (many of us make wrong choices and decisions not so much out of intent, as out of exhaustion!).

Jesus' invitation to His apostles came after He heard of *"all that they had done and taught."* It is not that they would be free of life's to-dos, but Jesus notes the need, and you should hear His invitation as one to you as well.

87

We are created to serve, but we are also created to rest. The Commandment, *"Remember the Sabbath,"* recalled six days of creation ended with one day of rest.[1] Rest is not just a commandment; it is an absolute necessity—without it, we collapse.

Every so often a national news story pops up about a sinkhole that has appeared in a populated area. As I understand it, sinkholes occur when underground streams drain away during seasons of drought. Eventually, the dry streambed causes the ground at the surface to lose its underlying support and suddenly everything begins to cave in. We have all seen photos of cars, sometimes homes, falling into sinkholes that have opened in what appeared to be stable places.

There are lots of people whose lives seem like one of these sinkholes. Most of us today have probably had the experience of feeling like we were on the verge of a cave-in of sorts...maybe you feel that way right now. There seems to be so much going on in your life that you feel like the ground is shifting beneath you; you cannot seem to get a handle on things. Maybe you thought doing more would clear space for more rest, but you find yourself just filling up the end of the list with more things to do—though you try and get a grip, the thing you thought might be a rope to pull you to safety is merely a string of sand slipping through your fingers. What's needed? Rest...a quiet and solitary place of stillness that brings about the kind of balanced harmony between what we do and who we are.

Engineers who design and build bridges test their strength by measuring their integrity—their ability to "hold up" under pressure. The strong foundation that rests beneath the bridge enables it to be what it was designed to be.

1   Exodus 20:8; Genesis 2:2.

Rest, quite frankly, restores integrity to our work—to our lives. The late Anne Morrow Lindbergh unveiled this well in a wonderful little book called *Gift from the Sea*. She wrote,

> But I want first of all—in fact, as an end to these other desires—to be at peace with myself. I want a singleness of eye, a purity of intention, a central core to my life that will enable me to carry out these obligations and activities as well as I can. I want, in fact—to borrow from the language of the saints—to live 'in grace' as much of the time as possible. I am not using this term in a strictly theological sense. By grace I mean an inner harmony, essentially spiritual, which can be translated into outward harmony. I am seeking perhaps what Socrates asked for in the prayer from the *Phaedrus* when he said, 'May the outward and inward man be at one.' I would like to achieve a state of inner spiritual grace from which I could function and give as I was meant to in the eye of God.[2]

An interesting sidebar in this reflection—one might say that Mark, the author of the Gospel that bears his name, reveals his own tendency to rush through life. Mark, likely written in the 60s A.D., is considered the earliest of the four Gospels and it is also the shortest! In many scenes he has things happening as if there is hardly a break between stories or events. He makes use of the word "immediately" no less than 40 times in his Gospel; perhaps this particular invitation of Jesus, in the midst of so many other things, left an impression on him.

Is your to-do list so long and the day so short that you are beginning to feel a bit like a sinkhole? Are you exhausted? Even God took a break! So put the to-dos down—take a breather—get some rest.

---

2   Anne Morrow Lindbergh, *Gift from the Sea*. (New York: Pantheon, Random House Books, 1975), pp. 23-24.

A New Leaf

You have probably read the old adage that one can choose to "work to live" or "live to work." Which do you do? The Christian pastor and preacher Vance Havner once wrote, "Jesus knows we must come apart and rest awhile, or else we may just plain come apart."[3] What can you stop doing right now to rest? What can you take off of your to-do list? What can wait? What can you simply remove from that list? Don't wait any longer.

A Prayer

O God of peace, who hast taught us that in returning and rest we shall be saved, in quietness and in confidence shall be our strength: By the might of thy Spirit lift us, we pray Thee, to Thy presence, where we may be still and know that thou art God; through Jesus Christ our Lord. *Amen.*[4]

---

3 Died 1986.
4 *The Book of Common Prayer*, p. 832.

For All the Right Reasons

*"While they were there, the time came for her to deliver
her child. And she gave birth to her firstborn son..."*

— Luke 2:6–7

Lest you think I might have leap-frogged over an important moment
in the changing of seasons between Old Testament and New, I
waited on Luke, the Gospels' historian, to lend us some insight here.
Luke was keen to get the story "right." He begins his Gospel with
these words,

> *"Since many have undertaken to set down an orderly account
> of the events that have been fulfilled among us, just as they
> were handed on to us by those who from the beginning were
> eyewitnesses and servants of the word, I too decided, after
> investigating everything carefully from the very first, to write
> an orderly account for you, most excellent Theophilus, so that
> you may know the truth concerning the things about which you
> have been instructed."[1]*

Luke, as you may know, also wrote one of our earliest "sequels," the
Book of Acts. He wanted to make sure his readers understood the
whole story, but he begins where Jesus' story begins—the Incarnation.
I once read an article suggesting the most powerful words in Mozart's
Requiem are these from the piece's ninth verse, *"Recordare, Jesu pie,/
Quod sum causa tuae viae."* The literal translation is *"Think, good Jesu,/
that I am the cause of your wondrous incarnation."[2]*

As we have already explored in much of the previous meditations,
humans just simply have the innate predisposition to disobey and

---

1 Luke 1:1–4. Note also, that a full reflection on the Incarnation is offered in my devotional, *Preparing Room.*
2 Christoph Wolff, *Mozart's Requiem: Historical and Analytical Studies* (Berkeley: University of California Press, 1994), p. 67.

disavow the Godness of God. We run from Him, but God continues to run after us. The Incarnation is the opening salvo of God's Gospel—His Good News—that though we are unrighteous, He is not. Though we are often taking the wrong road, He is constantly beckoning us back to the right one.

Jesus' birth opened the possibility that you and I could be made righteous despite our own unrighteousness (more on that a bit later). For now, is it not an incredible thing that the God of the universe chose to upend the Trinity and come to live among us as a child?

Though Luke gives the effort his all, there are so many things God "with us," Emmanuel, reveals that it is impossible to unveil all of them. But it says much, does it not, that God came not to impress with His intellect or wit or charm—He stepped into this world utterly and completely helpless. Nothing is more helpless than a baby! For the first two years of a baby's life, she or he is completely dependent on others for food, for care, for warmth.

He came as a babe, wrapped in bands of linen—swaddling clothes, Luke writes—and lay in a manger. We've dressed up that manger a bit since then, but a manger is not a stable, it is not a small barn. A manger is a feeding trough for cattle—that is where our God began His journey in this world. And as He entered helpless, He ended the same way. For as He died, He did so with no power left in Him—*"My God...My God...why have you forsaken me...It is finished,"* and He was taken down, and wrapped in linen cloths and laid in a borrowed tomb.

Why? Why helpless? Why not grand and big and loud and powerful? Because, if God came in this way, the powerless, the needy, the helpless would have felt disqualified—but He came helpless that we might know we could be helped by Him. Paul reminds the Christians in Corinth, *"For you know the generous act of our Lord Jesus Christ, that though he was rich, yet for your sakes he became poor, so that by his poverty you might become rich."*[3]

So, when all seems out of whack in your life...when things seem so far off base that you feel utterly helpless—without anywhere to turn to make things right—you have someone to whom you can go don't you? Who? *To the One who submitted, who allowed Himself to begin and end His journey in this world utterly dependent on the care of others—to the One who was born for all the right reasons.* That's worth clinging to—don't you think?

 ## A New Leaf

When autumn comes, Advent and Christmas are not too far away. There's much to dress up the incarnation story—but in the end, it is only about one divine motive—God's love for you. Maybe this year, as the decorations begin to appear at your local retailer, you can push back the loud cries of Christmas commercialism and acknowledge with Mozart the incredible truth that you—you are the cause for the coming of Jesus into the world.

---

3   II Corinthians 8:9.

A PRAYER

Lead me, O Spirit of God to the manger.

Not a manger of my own making, or thinking, or imagination; but to the manger wherein the baby Jesus lay.

Let me smell the wet hay, the sweat and steamy breath of cattle.

Let me feel the chill of the night, the rush of unwanted winds, the brittle warmth of bands of cloth.

May I see the tears of Mary and Joseph that well up and spill over lips that grin in joy, purse in wonder, tighten in fear for what may yet come.

Give me ears to hear the silence of shepherds who shuffle in from fields to behold the face of God.

Let me, O Spirit of God, taste the incarnation with all that I am; that I may be emptied of this world, and filled, filled with You. *Amen.*

Death for the Sake of Life

"Jesus answered them, 'The hour has come for the Son of Man to be glorified. Very truly, I tell you, unless a grain of wheat falls into the earth and dies, it remains just a single grain; but if it dies, it bears much fruit. Those who love their life lose it, and those who hate their life in this world will keep it for eternal life.'"

— John 12:23–25

Volumes have been written on the death of Jesus, so there is no need here to offer much more than the obvious. Jesus did come, as noted in the last devotion, out of God's love for us; but all that Jesus did and said put down the stepping stones to His crucifixion—His death on the cross for our sins. His death was not a good example; it was not merely revealing that God in Jesus was so good and so loving that He would die to prove a point. No, we are told throughout the Gospels—throughout the New Testament—that Jesus died, in Mark's telling *"to give his life a ransom for many."*[1]

John's Gospel, the fourth Gospel, was also written after Matthew, Mark and Luke—around 90 A.D. His poetic writing, different from the other Gospels, is a beautiful and horrible

---

1   Mark 10:45.

retelling of what his Gospel brothers had already written—that the shadow of the cross loomed over the crib in the manger. In this passage from John, Jesus let His disciples know that His "hour has come," and that His remaining days would take a decidedly deeper and more terrifying direction. Jesus' death, as He tells His followers here, is the moment that actually allows His power to do what it came to do.

We will unpack this more in some of the devotionals ahead, but let me borrow a bit from this season. While many of us typically associate spring with allergy season, I live in a part of the country now where fall brings allergies as well. In fact, I rarely had allergy issues until

I moved to Houston, but I have them now—aplenty—and the way out has been injections of antigens.

An allergy antigen is actually a small bit of the substance that makes you allergic; if you put a bit of this into you long enough, eventually it provokes immunity to the thing that was causing the reaction in the first place. Regular, consistent, exposure to the allergens has actually reduced their power over me, allowing my body to resist those things that seemed to be dominating my respiratory system.

This may be a stretch for some, but let me suggest that Jesus' death is the ultimate antigen for those things from which our souls suffer— sin, guilt and, yes, death. Jesus' death actually disarms the power of death over us—and the more we think on that, pray on that—the more we give ourselves over to the reality that Jesus did not just die because He was a nice guy trying to show others that self-sacrifice is a noble vocation. Jesus died so that you and I might live.

The Reverend Fleming Rutledge has put this powerfully, writing,

> Without the cross at the center of the Christian proclamation, the Jesus story can be treated as just another story about a charismatic spiritual figure. It is the crucifixion that marks out Christianity as something definitively different in the

history of religion. *It is in the crucifixion that the nature of God is truly revealed.* Since the resurrection is God's mighty transhistorical Yes to the historically crucified Son, we can assert that *the crucifixion is the most important historical event that has ever happened.*[2]

There is not one of us who does not desperately want the gifts offered through Jesus' death. Though we may, in our modern world, shrink back from the stark truths revealed in the Cross of Christ, it would be to our own detriment, for without Jesus' Cross, there would be no Christian faith. In fact, the promises of what rest beyond the grave would be null and void—death would mean death and nothing more. Yet it is more than that, isn't it? Heinrich Suso, a German Dominican friar, once wrote, "The cross possesses such power and strength that, whether they like it or not, it attracts and draws and carries away those who bear it."[3]

Through the lens of Jesus' death and our trust in that death, we are promised life—life abundant here and life yet to come, beyond death's sting. His death is, in fact, a death for life's sake—for your life's sake. Best to lay claim to that gift—for that is, in the end, what it is.

---

2   The Reverend Fleming Rutledge, *The Crucifixion: Understanding the Death of Jesus Christ* (Grand Rapids, Michigan: Eerdman's, 2015), p. 44.

3   Died 1366.

 *A New Leaf*

Alan M. Stibbs, a British evangelist, wrote, "This one event of the cross of Christ is a final revelation both of the character and consequence of human sin and the wonder and sacrifice of divine love."[4] Take some time today and reflect on the reasons "why" Jesus gave His life for you. Consider, then, how this shifts the Cross of Jesus from the tops of steeples and gravestones, from t-shirts and necklaces, to the very center of our faith. What can we do in the face of that truth but give our thanks?

A PRAYER

Rock of ages, cleft for me,
let me hide myself in thee;
let the water and the blood
from thy wounded side that flowed,
be of sin the double cure,
cleanse me from its guilt and power.

Should my tears forever flow,
should my zeal no languor know,
all for sin could not atone:
thou must save, and thou alone;
in my hand no price I bring,
simply to thy cross I cling.

While I draw this fleeting breath,
when mine eyelids close in death,
when I rise to worlds unknown
and behold thee on thy throne,
Rock of ages, cleft for me,
let me hide myself in thee.[5]
Amen.

---

4   Died 1971.
5   August Toplady (d. 1778). From *The Hymnal 1982* (New York: The Church Pension Fund, 1985), #685.

What "Raised" Means for You

"He is not here; for he has been raised, as he said."

— Matthew 28:6

As we press forward in our journey through scripture, I'm backing up a bit to Matthew's telling of Jesus' Resurrection. All four gospelers share different versions of this story, but there is something compelling about this little phrase spoken by an angel to the "Marys" who went to visit the tomb of the dead Jesus. When they arrived, the angel greeted them with these enduring words.

As the Christian faith is made impotent without the Cross of Christ, the Cross would have no meaning were it not for the Resurrection. Jesus' Resurrection confirmed, affirmed and validated everything He said and did during His life. Had Jesus not risen, then He clearly would have been remembered only as a wise and moral sage, a miracle worker who, like anyone else, breathed His last and returned to the earth as dust. But He was raised—and because He was, His story endures.

"He is not here..." means just that. Jesus, who three days before had been placed in a tomb, was dead—not swooned, not close to dead, not passed out—dead; a body beginning to grow stiff with rigor, not breathing, heart stopped, brain waves ceased, spirit/soul departed. The interesting factoid in John's version that when Jesus' dead body was pierced *"at once blood and water came out"* tells us (perhaps eons before modern science would have actually described what was going on) that the platelets in Jesus' blood were already

99

coagulating without the oxygen they needed and were separating from the watery plasma through which they normally flowed.[1] Dead.

"He has been raised..." means just that. The same creative force that breathed creation into "being" returned life to Jesus' new/resurrected body. A resurrected body—not resuscitated, not just "healed," not a "ghost"—but a resurrected, physical body that the apostles could touch, see and hear; a body that continued to teach, heal and even eat.[2] It was not a hallucination, as some modern philosophers, and sadly even Christian theologians, have suggested. Nor was it a hoax. All but two of the original apostles (Judas who took his own life and John, who died after many years in exile on the island of Patmos) gave their lives as martyrs for the "testimony" of the resurrection of Jesus Christ. I don't know about you, but I would not put my head under the blade for a hoax, hallucination or even a ghost.

"As he said..." The Resurrection of Jesus Christ was the *"Amen"* to everything else He said and did. He stands alone among the religious traditions of the world who made the claim that He was the Son of God come to bring salvation to the world—and that it would occur not just through a life well lived, lessons well taught and a sacrificial/ atoning death, but also—and most importantly—through the victory displayed in the resurrection.

It comes down to this: if Jesus was not raised from the dead, which He foretold that He would be, then everything else He said and did would be suspect, up for grabs; it would have no integrity whatsoever. As Anglican theologian, N.T. Wright has written,

> But the critical thing right from the beginning was that the resurrection of Jesus demonstrated that he was indeed the Messiah, that Jesus had indeed borne the destiny of Israel..., that He had gone through the climax of Israel's exile and had returned from that exile three days later according to and in fulfillment of the entire biblical narrative, and that His followers in being the witnesses to these things were thereby and thereupon commissioned to take the news of his victory to the ends of the earth.[3]

---

1   John 19:34.
2   John 21.
3   N.T. Wright, *The Challenge of Jesus* (Downer's Grove, Illinois: InterVarsity Press, 1999), p. 149.

Of course, if it is all true, then it has implications for us. A few years back, you may remember there was the suggestion of a scientific discovery that might very well have put an end to the Christian hope. A Hollywood producer (not an archaeologist, theologian, or clergyman, by the way) suggested a historic "find;" the possible "burial box" for a man named Jesus—alongside those of his mother, father and supposed wife. The suggestion, of course, was that such a find would be proof that Jesus did not "literally" rise from death. The problem with such a proposition is that ignores a very important piece of information.

The missing piece is the experience that millions upon millions in the last 2,000 years into our present day have had in some way of "meeting" this resurrected Lord—either through being touched by the Holy Spirit, or personal conversion, or the power of prayer, or the renewal offered by moral living, or the hope of forgiveness and mercy, or the gift of grace. All of these, and so many other pieces of "evidence," confirm that it happened, *as He said.*

And, of course, what this really means is that Easter does not have to be merely "back then and there," but can be "right now and here!" All the promises of Jesus don't stop with His last breath, or ours—He holds out the hope of resurrected life to all who will humbly acknowledge Him both as Lord and Savior. As William Temple, 98th Archbishop of Canterbury, wrote, "Fellowship with Christ is participation in the divine life which finds it fullest expression in triumph over death. Life is a larger word than resurrection; but resurrection is, so to speak, the crucial quality of life."

So, as we continue on our journey together this fall, may we take hold that Easter is not something that happens only in spring, only once a year—it is happening now and always for those who hear and welcome the news of Jesus' Resurrection. Do not see His rising from the grave as merely a kind of liturgical drama, but as a real, personal invitation to claim it for yourself; this is what the Risen Lord hoped, and hopes, for in the first place.

What does "raised" mean for you? Good news...in fact, the best news indeed—*"He is not here; for he has been raised, as he said."*

 A New Leaf

Is the Easter Story boxed in for you—holding only a place in the spring of your seasons? Ask Jesus, ask Him now to bring the good news of His Resurrection into your life right now. You may be facing your own stone-cold tomb, but Jesus' Resurrection is God's reminder that death, of any kind, does not have the last word. In the mighty hands of our Lord, the words "The End" never roll across the screen. Grab hold of that hope today.

A PRAYER

Jesus, our Lord, we praise you
that nothing could keep you dead in the grave.
You are stronger than death and the devil.
Help us to remember
that there is nothing to be afraid of,
because you are alive and by our side.[4]
Amen.

---

4 From *The Doubleday Prayer Collection*, Mary Batchelor, comp. (New York: Doubleday, 1996), p. 371.

A Fork in the Road

"Now as he was going along and approaching Damascus, suddenly a light from heaven flashed around him. He fell to the ground and heard a voice saying to him, 'Saul, Saul, why do you persecute me?' He asked, 'Who are you, Lord?' The reply came, 'I am Jesus, whom you are persecuting. But get up and enter the city, and you will be told what you are to do.'"

— Acts 9:3–6

I don't know about you, but when fall comes a rather significant shift takes place in my home. Summer clothes are put away, and sweaters, coats and heavier clothes come out of storage. Sometimes it is not until this annual ritual that I notice some clothes that worked last year are not going to stay with me into the future. Maybe a sweater was nibbled on by moths, or maybe I did not notice that stain on the shirt or irreparable tear in the pants when boxing them up for safe-keeping. In any case, what might have been was not going to be and I have to make a decision to let the past go.

Saul was faced with a similar though much more critical decision. We have all heard the phrase "Damascus Road experience," and the verse from Acts offers its origin. Saul had been a Jewish religious leader who was dead-set on crushing the growing body of Christ in the first century. He was present and clearly an instigator during the death of the first

Christian martyr, Stephen.[1] We are told in Acts that *"Saul approved of their killing him."*[2]

Then something happened. He was on task to continue his persecution of Jesus' followers, when on the road to Damascus he was blinded by a light. He fell to the ground and a risen Jesus spoke to him. *"Saul, Saul, why do you persecute me?"* A bit dumbfounded by the moment, Saul said, *"Who are you?"* Jesus told Saul that He is, in fact, the One Saul had been persecuting. It is here that Saul hit a fork in the road of his

 own life. At this meeting and in the days that followed, Saul would repent and relent, and become not just a follower of Christ, but an evangelist extraordinaire for Jesus and His Good News. His heart and life so shifted that soon he would take on another name, Paul—the apostle.[3]

The Book of Acts, as I noted earlier, was written by Luke. Luke was a physician and also missionary companion to Paul.[4] His book covers a time period from the 30s to 60s A.D. and very likely was written toward the close of that period, in the late 70s A.D.[5] It is filled with stories similar to Saul's/Paul's—people who were walking in one direction, following one path and then, when they encountered the Gospel story, chose a different way. The past did not necessarily disappear, but it no longer determined the future.

We probably all know people who have had these kinds of miraculous conversion turn-around moments; perhaps you are one. We probably also know people who say their experience of coming to follow Jesus was altogether different—perhaps bit by bit, over a long period of time. I have met some people who are so blessed to have the experience of never *not* knowing God in Christ.

Whatever the case, it is not so much *how* one comes to faith in Christ, but instead *that* they do. Saul had resisted the Gospel for a long time—so long that it made him a bitter religious zealot persecuting others for the sake of a past that no longer held his victims. But he too let

---

1 Acts 7:54–8:1.
2 Acts 8:1.
3 Acts 13:9.
4 See Colossians 4:14 and II Timothy 4:11.
5 No later than 84 A.D., the ascribed date of Luke's death.

go, and when he did—everything—*everything* changed. He became a loving, passionate advocate for Christ who would later testify to others, *"But I do not count my life of any value to myself, if only I may finish my course and the ministry that I received from the Lord Jesus, to testify to the good news of God's grace."*[6]

I think it is safe to say that somewhere, whether at the surface or deep down, one knows whether or not she or he resists God or walks with Him; one also knows how that came about. Few have given us more help with this than the Christian apologist, fiction writer, and professor of medieval literature than C.S. Lewis. After a long and strong resistance on his own part, he came to his own fork in the road and took it.

On May 22, 1929, Lewis wrote of his own Damascus Experience in converting to a belief in God,[7]

> You must picture me alone in that room in Magdalen, night after night, feeling, whenever my mind lifted even for a second from my work, the steady, unrelenting approach of Him of whom I so earnestly desired not to meet. That which I greatly feared had at last come upon me. In the Trinity Term of 1929 I gave in, and admitted that God was God, and knelt and prayed: perhaps, that night, the most dejected and reluctant convert in all England. I did not then see what is now the most shining and obvious thing; the Divine humility which will accept a convert even on such terms. The Prodigal Son at least walked home on his own feet. But who can duly adore that Love which will open the high gates to a prodigal who is brought in kicking, struggling, resentful, and darting his eyes in every direction for a chance of escape?...The hardness of God is kinder than the softness of men, and His compassion is our liberation.[8]

There comes a time when those who choose to follow Christ, indeed choose to do so—however they do it. They reach that fork in the road—where one road is a life without Christ and the other is a road with Him. They choose to walk with Him. The converted Paul would

---

6   Acts 20:24.
7   Lewis first converted to a belief in God and would have another conversion to the Christian faith in 1930.
8   C.S. Lewis, *Surprised by Joy* (Dorset: C.S. Lewis Pte. Ltd., 1955), Extract reprinted by permission.

years later describe it this way, *"You were taught to put away your former way of life, your old self...to be renewed in the spirit of your minds, and to clothe yourself with the new self, created according to the likeness of God."*[9] This is, I suppose, one way of saying "out with the old, in with the new." If the new way is the road with Christ, be assured, you are headed in the right direction.

 ## A New Leaf

May I be so bold as to invite you to consider which road you are on? If you are walking with our Lord, well then, take time today to give thanks for that journey. If you are not, perhaps you are at your own fork in the road—ask our Lord to come, take your hand and walk into the future together.

A PRAYER

Lord, be at my side now.
Give me courage to journey into the depth of my soul.
If I see You there, give me a grateful heart;
    and a generous one that I may share with others the Good News of Your love.
If I see You not, then may I pray, as Your followers have prayed for thousands of years;
"Come Lord Jesus, come, fill me and make me Yours,
this day, and evermore."
Amen.

---

9   Portions of Ephesians 4:22–24.

How to Live

"For in it the righteousness of God is revealed through faith for faith; as it is written, 'The one who is righteous will live by faith.'"

— Romans 1:17

I have lived south of Highway I-10 for more than two decades now. I-10 is a major highway that stretches from Santa Monica, California, to Jacksonville, Florida—and thus south means south. Fall and winter are not the same here as they are in most of the rest of our country. We experience our first freeze much later than most of the United States —if we have one at all. This year we did have a freeze and the end result on my relatively tropical garden was a bit disastrous. At least at first it seemed so.

I'll continue this theme in the next devotion, but one of the first impacts on my garden was the terminal illness and death of a cactus I had raised from a pup! The cactus' official name was *Pachycereus Marginatus*, often called a "Mexican fence post," or even more commonly a "column cactus" because it is simply tall and straight. When I bought it, it was about 24 inches high. It did not require much from me, but I was amazed how quickly it grew. In no time, it had reached my height of six feet. Not wanting to have our backyard mirror that of "H.I.'s" front yard from *Raising Arizona*, my wife

107

suggested we might ought to place it in a more private area—which meant the little garden outside my study, not seen by the public eye.

So, I put on my thick gloves and moved the little fella, thinking it would not survive the transplant. Not only did it survive, it grew... and grew...and grew some more. It endured a tumultuous move, a few harsh winter temperatures and not much attention from me. Before this freeze, it stood nearly 30 feet tall. In the spring, it would pop out pink fruity pods filled with seeds, and when summer came around, large yellow flowers would almost spurt from its sides. The freeze put an end to it all.

Our temperature dipped below 25 degrees (odd for us) and while I thought it might make it, I could see it had been frozen beyond repair. It began to wilt, then break apart. I finally had to don those gloves again, pull it out, and put it in the trash—gone for good. A bit melancholy was I. I had grown pretty used to its annual growth, blossoms and fruits. But the deep freeze meant its end and there was no use trying to revive a dead, old plant.

Long introduction—but here you go. The verse in this meditation from Romans is essentially the entire Christian life summed up in nine words, *"The one who is righteous will live by faith."*[1] As I pointed out in the last meditation, Paul had a Damascus Road moment when he came to see that a relationship with God is not about always getting it right; it is about a right relationship. But it is probably not a once-and-for-all kind of experience—Paul writes here that those who follow God in Christ do not just believe in what God has done for us in Christ, they actually "live" in it—and they do so, frankly, by faith.

To get a deeper handle on this, let us consider for a moment Martin Luther's own Damascus Road, which actually came as a fruit of this particular verse. Luther's conversion and breakthrough involved a correct understanding of God's righteousness. The phrase *"the righteousness of God is revealed"* had become the focal point of his frustrations with living fully into the Christian life. Luther had long struggled to blamelessly keep God's Law in order to become righteous. He believed this is what God demanded of him and all people. Time and again he failed to keep God's Law and achieve the righteousness that God demanded.

---

1   See also Genesis 15:6; Habakkuk 2:4; note, though I have referenced this touchstone already in Meditations 3 and 19, I **press** the point here again to show the consistency of this message throughout Holy Scripture.

All this came to a head as he was wrestling with this passage. He would honestly confess that he was extremely zealous to understand Romans but that this phrase about God's righteousness stood in the way. Why? Because the phrase *"the righteousness of God"* like most Biblical terms (such as grace, faith, justification, etc.) had been reinterpreted by scholastic theologians of the high and late Middle Ages 1100–1500 A.D. to support a theology of law and works. For centuries the Church had taught that the righteousness of God was God's active, personal righteousness or justice by which He punishes the unrighteous sinner.

Luther bought into this and it became deeply imbedded in his psyche. Therefore whenever he came across the phrase *"the righteousness of God"* in Scripture, it terrified him –in his words—they "struck my conscience like lightning" and felt "like a thunderbolt in my heart" because he knew that he was an unrighteous sinner who fell far short of God's righteous (perfect) demands.

Even worse, Romans 1:17 filled Luther with anger and hatred toward God. "I did not love, yes, I hated the righteous God who punishes sinners." Is it not enough, Luther tells us he murmured, that God crushes us miserable sinners with His law, but also God has to threaten us with punishment through the gospel, too?

After meditating day and night, finally the breakthrough came when Luther gave heed to the words at the end of 1:17, *"The one who is righteous shall live by faith."* Then he realized that the verse was not talking about the active righteousness that God demands, but the passive righteousness that He freely gives to those who believe the Gospel. The sinner is justified (declared righteous) by God through faith in the work and death of Jesus, not by our work or keeping of the Law. Put another way, the sinner is justified by receiving (faith) rather than achieving (works). Later Luther would say that we are saved by the alien righteousness of Christ, not by a righteousness of our own doing.

He called this his "tower experience" and according to Luther it was a conversion moment. When he had discovered that God gives His righteousness as a gift in Christ, he felt that he "was altogether born again and had entered paradise itself through open gates...that place in Paul was for me truly the gate to paradise." Then his conscience was at rest and he was certain of his salvation. Before there had been only unrest and uncertainty.

Let me circle back to that old, dead cactus. When it died, it was dead—there was no in-between. I was not going to revive it, no matter what I did. I finally had to admit that it was no longer to be part of my garden.

What Paul would spend much of his life preaching and writing about was the uselessness of trying to win God's love through what we do. There is no in-between—either God loves us because of who we are or He loves us because of what we do. If it is because of what we do—we will never—NEVER—have a sense of peace in this life. We will spend the rest of our lives wondering if we will "make the cut." On the other hand, if we realize that God loves us because He created us to be loved, and when we had fallen into sin and death sent His own Son to tend to that with His death and resurrection—when we hold fast to that, by believing God's goodness is infinitely better and more than our badness, well, then—we can live, live in peace, live as children of God.

As a priest, I have people ask me all the time about how they should live; and the older I get, the more I realize, we live by faith—we live by trusting in Jesus Christ—who He was, who He is, what He did, and what He is doing in and through us.

The Very Rev. Philip Pare, an Anglican priest who died in 1992, was a wise and deep man of faith. Before his death, he penned these words,

> Very often, when people first turn toward God and realize that God loves them and that everything about them matters to Him, a wave of joyful emotion overwhelms them. But actual faith is mostly the realization that, even though we don't in the least deserve it, God believes in us and finds us loveable. This is astonishing.

How to live? We live by faith—and, well, this is astonishing, indeed.

 ## A New Leaf

Does Luther's story resonate with you? Do you have a burden wherein you feel as though you never, never measure up? Is it time to root out of your life the death that comes with believing you are loved by God because of what you do, and instead allow something new to be born—faith—faith which embraces a hope that you are loved by God because—well, He loves you? It might be time to take something to the garbage heap! What do you think?

A PRAYER

Jesus, how sweet is the very thought of you! You fill my heart with joy. The sweetness of your love surpasses the sweetness of honey. Nothing sweeter than you can be described; no words can express the joy of your love. Only those who have tasted your love for themselves can comprehend it. In your love you listen to all my prayers, even when my wishes are childish, my words confused, and my thoughts foolish. And you answer my prayers, not according to my own misdirected desires, which would bring only bitter misery; but according to my real needs, which bring me sweet joy. Thank you, Jesus, for giving yourself to me. *Amen.*

— Bernard of Clairvaux, d. 1153

Pruning It to the Core

*"For I decided to know nothing among you
except Jesus Christ, and him crucified."*

— I Corinthians 2:2

Let me hover just a bit more on what the freeze did to the few flora in my garden. We have a lush Meyer lemon tree in our yard. It is not huge, but for some reason, where it is and the amount

of sun, water and soil must be just right—one year the harvest was an amazing 500 or so huge, yellow lemons.

They are quite tasty—not too sour or sweet. We use the juice in home recipes; we give them away as presents; and I use the juice in handmade soaps that I craft from time to time.

Unfortunately, the freeze that took out the cactus also hit that lemon tree hard. Within a week or so, when temperatures returned to normal, virtually every single leaf fell off the tree. We thought it was, like the cactus, a goner for sure.

But a good friend who is also an arborist cautioned against despair. He said when we were fairly sure the freezes were over, it would be obvious which branches would no longer bear fruit and which would. At that time, he said, "prune it back." I trusted my friend on this, followed his direction, and pruned several dead and dying limbs off. When spring returned, lo and behold, the leaves burst out as they never before had. The tree had basically come back to life because the pieces not worth saving had been trimmed away.

As a priest, I am often asked, "What is the essential message of the Gospel?" That can be challenging, because there is much to the Christian faith. For instance, I think it is fair to say that Jesus pointed not to a myriad of commandments when asked which was the most important. He suggested, above all others, two: *"You shall love the Lord your God with all your heart, and with all your soul, and with all your strength, and with all your mind; and your neighbor as yourself."*[1] Jesus was not suggesting the other commandments in the Bible are not important or are to be disregarded; instead, He was simply saying that of all the ones there are—these two are the most important. These two "sum up" the Law.

If one were to ask, "What is the most important Christian ethic?" Some might point to the poetry of Paul's reflection on loving others that we find in I Corinthians 13, for he notes here that above all other actions of the Christ follower, *"the greatest of these is love."*[2] Paul was not suggesting other actions of the Christian (for instance, charity, hospitality, kindness and so on) are not also to be part of the Christian's life; it was simply to say, above all actions a Christian can take, no action trumps love.

In a sense, Jesus and Paul in these two examples were "pruning" the message down to the core. In the passage from I Corinthians 2:2, Paul does the same with the basic Christian message. Throughout the Corinthian correspondence, Paul tells the Corinthians many things. While Paul was teaching and preaching in Corinth during his missionary season there, he no doubt said many things.[3] But later, when in Ephesus, word reaches him that there is a great deal of division in the Church in Corinth, over a great many things.

Paul does address those things, but here in this passage he prunes it down to the core, *"The most important thing is Jesus and him crucified."* While I have already touched on the death of Jesus, we can take to heart here an important touchstone. From what we know, Jesus died around 30 A.D. (give or take a year) and this portion of the Corinthian correspondence was written about 25 years later. Yet already the

1   Luke 10:27; cf. Deuteronomy 6:5 and Leviticus 19:18; see Meditation 5.
2   I Corinthians 13:13.
3   Paul was in Corinth beginning roughly 51 A.D.; his missionary journey there is referenced in Acts 18.

113

early Christians were forgetting that the Cross was the bedrock and foundation of the Church—nothing more and certainly nothing less. Those of us who live, and worship, and are nourished by the truth, may find lots of things that help us along our Christian journey—but at the core of all that we are as Christians, we need to remember that we worship a God not removed from the suffering of the world, but one who stepped right into it.

What this means is that everything we know of our faith is to be filtered through Jesus' death on the Cross. Remove the death of Jesus, and one removes all that Jesus came and did.

P.T. Forsyth, an English Congregationalist, wrote, "Christ is to us just what His cross is. All that Christ was in heaven or on earth was put into what He did there...Christ, I repeat, is to us just what His cross is. You do not understand Christ till you understand His cross."[4]

Anglican Bishop Stephen Neill makes this point as well, writing, "In the Christian theology of history, the death of Christ is the central point of history, here all the roads of the past converge; hence all the roads of the future diverge."[5]

So Paul reminds the Corinthians here, as he does you and me, that part of our journey is to prune away anything that takes away from the core message of Christian theology—Jesus Christ and His Cross.[6] Why is it so important to understand this?

Several decades ago, I was fortunate to travel to the tiny province of Macao, just near the border of the People's Republic of China. It was above a harbor there that centuries ago Portuguese settlers built an enormous cathedral. They believed it would weather time and they placed on its front a massive bronze cross that stood high into the sky. Some

---

4   P.T. Forsyth, *The Cruciality of the Cross*, (London: Forgotten Books, 2012), pp. 44–45.
5   From, "Jesus and History," in *Truth of God Incarnate*, ed. E.M.B. Green (Grand Rapids: Eerdman's, 1977), p. 80.
6   Perhaps no two better books in the last few decades have been written on the meaning and purpose of the Cross than John Stott's *The Cross of Christ* and the Reverend Fleming Rutledge's *The Crucifixion: Understanding the Death of Jesus Christ*.

years later, a typhoon swept away the cathedral and it was pushed down the hill as debris and into the ocean—except the front wall and that bronze cross still stood high.

A few centuries after that, there was a shipwreck out a little beyond that same harbor. In the wreck some died and some lived, but one of the survivors was hanging onto wreckage from the ship. Moving up and down in the ocean as the swells were moving, he was disoriented, frightened and did not know where land was. As he would come up on the swell, he would spot that cross, tiny from that distance. His name was Sir John Bowring. When he made it to land, and lived to tell the story, he penned a hymn well known to us,

> In the Cross of Christ I glory,
> towering o'er the wrecks of time;
> all the light of sacred story
> gathers round its head sublime.
>
> When the woes of life o'er take me,
> hopes deceive, and fears annoy,
> never shall the cross forsake me;
> It glows with peace and joy.[7]

John Bowring reminds the Christian that when all of life seems to crush in on top of us, we need to go back to the Cross, remember the empty tomb, and call to mind the fact that the Jesus of our faith is neither on the cross nor in the tomb, but that He lives and stands ready, and is able to give us victory through whatever we are going through at the time. Sickness, disease, peer pressure, stress, job loss, brokenness, divorce, sin, guilt, cancer, death—through the lens of the Cross, none of these are the last word.

Indeed, Jesus' death on the Cross defeated death and the powers of death in this world. In that Cross of Christ—we glory.

---

7   John Bowring (d. 1872). From *The Hymnal 1982* (New York: The Church Pension Fund, 1985), #441.

A New Leaf

Where do you place the Cross of Jesus in your own personal Christian journey? Has it been lost in stained glass, prayer books, the latest Christian book or charismatic speaker? It is not that other things than the Cross are not important, or cannot help us in our Christian walk, but they are not, essentially, the heart of the Christian message. Spend some time today pondering the Cross of Jesus...perhaps there are things that need to be pruned away so that the Cross can take its rightful place in your own Christian life—at the very center.

A PRAYER

When I survey the wondrous cross
Where the young Prince of glory died,
my richest gain I count but loss,
and pour contempt on all my pride.

Forbid it, Lord, that I should boast,
save in the cross of Christ my God;
all the vain things that charm me most,
I sacrifice them to his blood.[8]
Amen.

— Isaac Watts, d. 1784

---

8   Isaace Watts (d. 1748). From *The Hymnal 1982* (New York: The Church Pension Fund, 1985), #474.

The Promise of the Unseen

"So we do not lose heart. Even though our outer nature is wasting away, our inner nature is being renewed day by day. For this slight momentary affliction is preparing us for an eternal weight of glory beyond all measure, because we look not at what can be seen but at what cannot be seen; for what can be seen is temporary, but what cannot be seen is eternal."

— II Corinthians 4:16–18

Let me stretch out this story on the pruning of that lemon tree just a bit more. My hope in pruning was that the effort might restore what very much appeared to be dead, to life—and lo and behold, it did!

The passage above from II Corinthians is part of a larger reflection by the apostle Paul on the challenges brought by the fragility of this life in the hope that the promise of eternal life can breathe into that fragility.[1] I have used this passage as inspiration for dozens of homilies at funeral services over the years.

The desperation that one could face if what is "seen" is all there is would mean that this life we have would be staggeringly void of meaning and purpose. I am a great admirer of one of our founding fathers, Thomas Jefferson. He was a man of incredible creativity. You may know his little book, *The Jefferson Bible,* his own version of the gospel. In it, he carved out bits and pieces of Jesus' life—anything that might be considered miraculous—because he found it impossible to believe in the miracles. He named his miracle-free version *The Life and Morals of Jesus of Nazareth*. This founding father

---

1   The full passage begins at II Corinthians 4:1 and continues through 5:10. I commend it to your reading in the context of this meditation.

was not a Christian, he was a Unitarian, if that, and he ends his little version of the Gospels in this way, *"Then took they the body of Jesus, and wound it in linen clothes with spices, as the manner of the Jews is to bury. Now, in the place where he was crucified, there was a garden; and in the garden a new sepulcher, wherein was never man yet laid. There laid they Jesus, And rolled a great stone to the door of the sepulcher, and departed."*[2]

None of us knows, I suppose, if Jefferson ever embraced what the resurrection of Jesus could mean in one's day-to-day life, but Paul had it through and through. The Corinthian Christians, like you and me, had to deal with the reality that this life, as we know it, does not last forever.

He would compare our bodies to tents—temporary resting places for who we are—but, as he points out, there waits for the children of God something more.

So, when crisis strikes, health declines, life's regular challenges arise— Paul's counsel is to remember they are temporary; they will not last forever, and that should be a source of courage and strength to live life fully until it is time to leave this tent and go to our eternal home.

You may know the story of Joni Eareckson Tada. At age 17, her life changed dramatically when she dove into a shallow lake and suffered a spinal cord fracture that left her paralyzed from the neck down, without the use of her hands and legs. Lying in a hospital bed, she tried desperately to make sense of the horrible turn of events. She begged friends to assist in her suicide. Anything to end her misery.

She says she believed in God, but she was so angry with Him. How could this circumstance be a demonstration of His love and power? Surely He could have stopped it from happening. How could permanent, lifelong paralysis be part of His loving plan?

But a good friend of Joni pointed her to Christ. He reminded her that Christ suffered and pointed her to the promises of Christ's companionship in that suffering. In time, Jesus would turn over the

---

2   Thomas Jefferson, *The Jefferson Bible: The Life and Morals of Jesus of Nazareth* (Boston: Beacon Press, 1989), pp. 146–147.

stone of Joni's suffering, "Now," she says, "I believe that God's purpose in my accident was to turn a stubborn kid into a woman...My wheelchair used to symbolize alienation and confinement. But God has changed its meaning because I have trusted in Him. Now my wheelchair symbolizes independence. It is a choice I made and one that anyone can make...I used to think happiness was a Friday night date, a size 12 dress, and a future with Ethan Allen furniture and 2.5 children. Now I know better. What matters is love."

She has made it no secret that though Christ has been a close companion in her suffering, there have been times of great darkness and depression. One of those traveled right along with her into an Episcopal Church on an Easter morning some years ago. Carrying a stone of depression along, she still came to church, hoping no doubt something said or sung or done in the service would turn her life around. She then heard the prayer assigned for that Easter Sunday: *"Almighty God, who through thine only-begotten Son Jesus Christ hast overcome death and opened unto us the gate of everlasting life: Grant that we, who celebrate with joy the day of the Lord's resurrection, may be raised from the death of sin by thy life-giving Spirit; through the same Jesus Christ our Lord."*[3]

With those words sinking beyond ear to heart, she began to weep. She began to have a vision of what rests beyond the grave. She says she suddenly realized that when this life is over and she arrives at the wedding feast of the Lamb of God, she will first fall down on her knees before Jesus. Then, then she says, she will stand—stand on her own two feet, freed from the wheelchair, released from the paralysis of arms and legs, and she will dance.

Joni's story reminds us that no trial on earth has the final word on the outcome of our stories—that handing the "deaths" of this world over to the power of God's Son is at the same time relinquishing it into the hands of the One who rose from death itself.

---

3   Collect for Easter Day, *The Book of Common Prayer*, Gregory Michael Howe, Custodian (New York: Oxford University Press, 2006), pp. 170-171.

What death are you facing this day? Turn your eyes from that grave toward the hope offered in the resurrection of Jesus Christ and the resurrection promised to God's children. Fix your eyes not on what is seen but what is unseen, and then join with Paul's proclamation to the ancient Corinthian Christians, *"Where, O death, is your victory? Where, O death, is your sting?"*[4]

 A New Leaf

We all know the saying that sometimes you cannot see the forest for the trees. When the challenges of life—in whatever form they come—come crashing down, it is easy to feel abandoned, alone, hopeless. But whatever we face, the promises of our faith tell us we have a God who will never forsake us. I love those words of Corrie Ten Boom, "There is no pit so deep, that God's love is not deeper still."

Invite Christ into whatever despair you face this day. You know, for a while, I thought that lemon tree was dead as a proverbial doornail—how wrong I was! There's often hope in the unseen. Turn the eyes of your heart in that direction and just see what God will do

---

4   I Corinthians 15:55.

A Prayer

I lift up my eyes to the hills—
    from where will my help come?
My help comes from the Lord,
    who made heaven and earth.
He will not let your foot be moved;
    he who keeps you will not slumber.
He who keeps Israel
    will neither slumber nor sleep.
The Lord is your keeper;
    the Lord is your shade at your right hand.
The sun shall not strike you by day,
    nor the moon by night.
The Lord will keep you from all evil;
    he will keep your life.
The Lord will keep your going out and your coming in
    from this time on and forevermore.
Amen.

— Psalm 121

Lawless Fruits

"The fruit of the Spirit is love, joy, peace, patience, kindness, generosity, faithfulness, gentleness, and self-control. There is no law against such things."

— Galatians 5:22–23

One of the things I have learned about tending to fruit trees is that one cannot hurry the process. In addition to the lemon tree in our yard, my wife and I are fortunate to have orange, lime and grapefruit

trees. We have no say in how many fruits will come from each tree, and again, because of our climate, we don't have much say in when they might pop out—these trees (when not blasted by a deep freeze) seem to be producing fruits year 'round. Our task? Stand back and let the soil, water and sun do the work.

Paul's letter to the Church in Galatia, like most of his other letters, touches on a number of points. Much like the Christians in Corinth, the Galatian followers of Christ had gotten confused about the essentials of the faith. Paul moves from downright frustration (at one point writing, *"You foolish Galatians! Who has bewitched you?"*)

to gentle reminders *("In Christ Jesus you are all children of God through faith.")*.[1] In a word, the Galatians were creeping back to the law and forgetting about grace.

They had, as a result of Paul's preaching and time with them, learned that, as I have already noted, righteousness is the result of a right relationship with God.[2] On this point, the Galatians are not far removed from many modern followers of Christ. The Church and its preachers have often been guilty of preaching grace but expecting a particular code of behavior and conduct. When one can point to his or her own achievements, there is a sense of satisfaction—of personal accomplishment. But when we do that in relationship to our own righteousness, then it invalidates Jesus' salvific work on our behalf.

So Paul attempts to reboot their computers—don't try and attain righteousness on your own! Cling to Christ, and let Him work out His righteousness in and through you. What does that look like? Paul said the followers of Christ would naturally bear fruits. The list is in the meditation verse. Often called the nine-fold fruits, Paul's point was you can't really "try" and produce these attributes on your own; they can only be borne within you when the conditions are right, much like the fruits on the trees in our little garden.

Look at that list of fruits. Have you ever tried to be at peace? How long does that last? Have you attempted to be patient or gentle? What happens when you get in the long line at the grocery? Have you successfully practiced self-control? Have you found what a friend of mine often says, "What you resist, persists!"

Paul's counsel is to see it a different way altogether. If you want the fruits of God to be present in your life, don't work to produce them—give yourself to God and let Him take it from there. I once read a sermon in which the preacher wisely suggested,

> We don't need to pray for more patience, we don't need to pray for more love, we don't need to pray for more joy and we don't need to pray for more kindness. We need to pray for more Jesus. For more of the Spirit.[3]

---

1   Galatians 3:1, 3:26.
2   For reference's sake, Paul twice visited Galatia, on his second missionary journey, 49 A.D., cf. Acts 16:6; returning on his third missionary journey, 53 A.D., cf. Acts 18:23. This letter may very well have been written between these two journeys.
3   From an article entitled, "Innovating to Zero Sin," in *Homiletics*, Timothy E. Merrill, Executive Editor (Beaufort, South Carolina, March-April, 2017), p. 43.

That is some very good counsel—and it was precisely Paul's point. Pray not to be good, or better or even best—just pray for the presence of Jesus and His Spirit in your life. For lack of a better phrase—"plant yourself in Christ," stand back and let Him take it from there. In time, you'll see law-free fruits popping out all over, not fruits of your own making, but of God's—how about that?

 ## A New Leaf

Do you find yourself trying to be good and yet feeling like you'll just never get there? That burden can, in no time, feel like a prison with no possibility of escape. Paul also wrote to the Galatians, *"For freedom Christ has set us free. Stand firm, therefore, and do not submit again to a yoke of slavery."[4]* The Gospel of grace—the essence of Christianity—is that we find goodness by the presence of God in our lives. That is a truth that, in Jesus' words, *"will make you free."[5]* Take some time to consider planting yourself more firmly in Christ—give Him the time and space in your heart to bring about the fruits of the Spirit. It will set you free indeed.

A PRAYER

Christ be with me, Christ within me,
Christ behind me, Christ before me,
Christ beside me, Christ to win me,
Christ to comfort and restore me. [6]
Amen.

— Attributed to St. Patrick of Ireland

---

4   Galatians 5:1.
5   John 8:32.
6   A firm date for the life and death of St. Patrick cannot be set, though it is generally agreed he carried out his missionary work in the second half of the 5th century A.D. This prayer is well known, but this version is taken from Michael Mitton's *The Soul of Celtic Spirituality In the Lives of its Saints* (Mystic, Connecticut: Twenty-Third Publications, 1996), p. 134.

Giving the Devil His Due

"Do not make room for the devil."

— Ephesians 4:27

A confession here—I'm a Halloween fan. With the first cold snap of fall, the first few falling leaves, the shorter days, my mind turns to happy memories as a child of decorating my home, dressing in a Spiderman costume or donning a sheet with a few holes cut out for eyes, and hitting the streets with my sisters and friends to load up on more candy any person has a right to consider consuming. Over the years, I have enjoyed watching classic horror movies (for the record— "classic," not the gore-ridden modern slasher movies). As a child, I built Aurora monster models based on those classic movies. If there's a haunted house at the amusement park, I'll take my place in line. It may be the excitement of the spooky settings and stories; I cannot fully explain it.

As a child of the south, there was a fairly thick dividing line amongst Christians and Halloween. Some took it all in good fun, others saw a clear and direct connection to evil, and still others fell somewhere in between.

A bit of historical context first: *Halloween* or *Hallowe'en* (a contraction of All Hallows' Evening), also known as *Allhalloween, All Hallows' Eve* or *All Saints' Eve*, is a rather ancient celebration traditionally held on October 31, the night before *All Hallow's Day* or *All Saints' Day* (more on that in the next meditation). Throughout the history of the Church, it was traditional for some believers to hold all-night vigils before major feast days in the Church. For instance, Christmas Eve was before Christmas Day, Shrove Tuesday before Ash Wednesday and Holy Saturday before Easter Sunday. The all-night vigil before All Saints' Day was also observed in this way as some western Christians visited the graves of loved ones by night and offered prayers of thanksgiving and memory. It is not a stretch for one to see how this practice evolved into the purely secular practice of Halloween.

However, in the late 1960s, the Satanic Church announced that Halloween was, in fact, one of its major holidays (noteworthy, December 24 is as well). But evil, demons and the devil are no modern innovations. For Christians, there's something to knowing something about evil.

In the preface of his keenly-crafted work on evil, *The Screwtape Letters*, C.S. Lewis wisely counsels,

> There are two equal and opposite errors into which our race can fall about the devils. One is to disbelieve in their existence. The other is to believe, and to feel an excessive and unhealthy interest in them. They themselves are equally pleased by both errors...[1]

We've certainly witnessed both throughout history. The Spanish Inquisition and Salem Witch Trials are examples of satanic obsession gone awry. You and I practice a hold-over from the past every time we say "God bless you" to someone who sneezes—for the origin of that blessing was the belief that you had just expelled a demon with your sneeze!

We can also easily underestimate the reality and power of evil. As Lewis suggests, to ignore the reality of evil is to empower it. After decades of pastoral ministry, I have personally witnessed this power particularly in and through the lives of those who have been abused in any way. Would anyone look on the horrors of Auschwitz, the killing fields of Cambodia, the terrorist attacks of September 11, 2001, or the vicious torture and executions carried out by ISIS since its birth in 1999 and say these are not, in some way, the fruit of pure evil?

Of course, when evil is this blatant it is easily identifiable. As Christ-followers, it would behoove us to remember that the devil has but one

1   C.S. Lewis, *The Screwtape Letters* (New York: HarperOne, 1996), p. 1X.

goal—to keep us from knowing the love and saving power of Christ. Toward that end, it is not always as easy to identify as something that goes bump in the night.

Back to Lewis for a moment. *The Screwtape Letters* were in fact a fictional collection of letters crafted by C.S. Lewis of a senior demon counseling a junior demon in the craft of temptation. While fiction, the book holds some solid truths. At one point the senior demon, Screwtape, writes to his apprentice, Wormwood,

> The fact that "devils" are predominantly *comic* figures in the modern imagination will help you. If any faint suspicion of your existence begins to arise in his mind, suggest to him a picture of something in red tights, and persuade him that since he cannot believe in that (it is an old textbook method of confusing them) he therefore cannot believe in you.[2]

And here's another quote from Screwtape to Wormwood,

> When he goes inside [the church], he sees the local grocer with rather an oily expression on his face bustling up to offer him one shiny little book containing a liturgy which neither of them understands, and one shabby little book containing corrupt texts of a number of religious lyrics, mostly bad, and in very small print...Make his mind flit to and fro between an expression like "the body of Christ" and the actual faces in the next pew...Provided that any of those neighbors sing out of tune, or have boots that squeak, or double chins, or odd clothes, the patient will quite easily believe that their religion must...therefore be somehow ridiculous...Keep everything hazy in his mind now...[3]

What's the point here? The point is to give the devil his due but make no room for him in your life. However you wish to interpret the devil and evil in the world, it is likely not going to be found under the masks of a congregation of costumed children with open bags waiting for a bit of candy. It is, frankly, more likely to be found in

2   C.S. Lewis, *The Screwtape Letters* (New York: HarperOne, 1996), p. 32.
3   C.S. Lewis, *The Screwtape Letters* (New York: HarperOne, 1996), pp. 5–7.

very unexpected places—dressed in whispers that are hiding gossip, or judgment in the disguise of righteousness, or greed in the costume of consumption—or even terrorism carried out in the name of God. Peter wisely warned the early Christians, *"Discipline yourselves, keep alert. Like a roaring lion your adversary the devil prowls around, looking for someone to devour."*[4]

As Paul warned the Christians in Ephesus, don't give the devil a foothold...be wise...be watchful...don't be afraid to name evil as evil—and more important than that—don't be afraid. We know how the story ends. God turns evil on its head. Maybe that's one reason evil, spelled in reverse, is *live*.

 ## A New Leaf

What's your take on evil? The devil? Demons? Have you underestimated these powers and principalities? Have you overestimated them? There are two pieces of traditional baptismal services that are worth revisiting.

Candidates for baptism are asked, "Do you renounce Satan and all the spiritual forces of wickedness that rebel against God?" The baptismal candidate is to respond, "I renounce them."

Later in the service, everyone in attendance who is a Christian is asked "Will you persevere in resisting evil, and, whenever you fall into sin, repent and return to the Lord?" The response for those who agree is "I will, with God's help."[5]

Are these questions worth pondering today? Either way, know this: the way forward is "with God's help." Perhaps, today, ask for it in defeating any demons you may encounter.

---

4   I Peter 5:8.
5   "Holy Baptism," in *The Book of Common Prayer*, p. 302 and 304.

A Prayer

Lord Jesus You taught us to pray, "Deliver us from evil."
So I do...
deliver me from evil in all its forms...
deliver me from ignoring evil...
deliver me when I have aided evil...
deliver me when I succumb to evil...
deliver me when I have been evil...
deliver me from fear of evil...
and finally Lord, in Your mercy...
protect and defend me...
      and those I love...
            and those You love...
                from evil...
In the power of Your Name, Jesus...
      I pray.
Amen.

A Song Worth Singing

"Paul and Timothy, servants of Christ Jesus, to all the saints in Christ Jesus..."

— Philippians 1:1

In 1929, a woman named Lesbia Scott published a song that has grown to be the one of the most famous of hymns sung, particularly on November 1, *All Saints' Day*. Its simple words utter an important truth,

> I sing a song of the saints of God,
> patient and brave and true,
> who toiled and fought and lived and died,
> for the Lord they loved and knew.

> And one was a doctor, and one was a queen,
> and one was a shepherdess on the green:
> They were all of them saints of God –
> and I mean, God helping, to be one too.

And then the final words...

> They live not only in ages past,
> there are hundreds of thousands still,
> the world is bright with the joyous saints
> who love to do Jesus' will.

> You can meet them in school, or in lanes or at sea,
> in church, or in trains, or in shops, or at tea,
> for the saints of God are just folk like me,
> and I mean to be one too.[1]

---

1   Lesbia Scott (d. 1986). From *The Hymnal 1982* (New York: The Church Pension Fund, 1985), #293.

I suspect your average Christian might hit the pause button here and say, "Saints? Me? A saint? Aren't saints special folk...holy folk...like Mary, John, Paul, Teresa?" Well, yes—they are saints, but if you are a follower of Christ, according to our faith—you, too, are a saint, and All Saints' Day belongs not just to the well-known saints of ages past, but the not-so-well-known saints of today.

Clearly that is what the apostle Paul and his young friend Timothy believed when together they wrote to the church in Philippi. It was addressed not to *"the most important saints"* or *"the most holy saints"* or only to *"some saints,"* but instead to *"all the saints in Christ Jesus."*

This letter, written in the early 60s A.D. is, frankly, a happy letter. The believers—saints—in Philippi were a source of great joy for Paul. In fact, this letter is called "The Joyful Letter," as variations of the word joy are used more than 15 times in its four short chapters. Even though the apostle Paul was apparently imprisoned (verse 13), the letter spills over with gratitude for these saints in Philippi.

While the origins of All Saints' Day stretch back to the earliest centuries of the Church, when believers who had died and gone to be with our Lord were remembered in prayers of thanksgiving, it is now a double reminder—not just of who has gone before, but of who we are—you and I, as followers of Jesus. And we need days like All Saints'. Why?

A few years back, Nicholas Sparks wrote a novel entitled *The Notebook*, which was eventually made into a rather popular film. The movie starts off with an old man in a nursing home reading a story from a tattered notebook to an elderly woman. He does this day after day. At first, she seems hesitant to have this visit from a stranger, but as he begins to read, she always tells him to "go on."

The Notebook tells the story of Allie and Noah's romantic courtship—the ups and downs, strains and celebrations, and eventually their marriage and life together. In time, you learn that the notebook is actually the elderly woman's own story about her life with this very man—the man reading the story to her—a story she herself wrote, but cannot remember because she suffers with Alzheimer's disease.

Then the moment comes for which Noah has been waiting—Allie's eyes almost awaken and she says, "How long do we have?" Noah replies, "We had five minutes last time." "I want to dance," Allie says, "hold me close once again." Slipping out of her memory loss for a gift of only moments, she remembers who Noah is—who they are. Noah takes her in his arms and they slowly dance—a picture of recovery of self at last, of coming home again, of peace found.[2]

You know, God knows we have memory troubles. Sometimes it is literal—old age, dementia, Alzheimer's. Difficult as they are, we know they are part of reality for some. But we can also suffer from a kind of spiritual Alzheimer's. That is why much of the Judeo-Christian story is not just story, but story told to remind us who we are and who we are called to be.

All Saints' Day is just such a reminder. It is a day when we remember the great saints like Martin, or Francis, or Martha or Elizabeth, or saints who may be known to you alone—your grandmother, a teacher, a coach, a friend. All Saints' Day is a day to remember and give thanks for those saints.

It is also a reminder of who we are called to be—and who, in God's eyes, we actually are. Saints are not perfect; saints are those who are part of the family of Jesus Christ. They are, as the song goes, from all walks of life and you can meet them about anywhere, including in the mirror.

You may also recall a movie entitled *Cinderella Man* based on the true story of boxing legend James Braddock. Injured and arthritic,

Braddock's promising career was cut short and he had to go on public assistance when he could not get work at the docks in New Jersey during the Depression. But when the opportunity came to get back in the ring to provide a living for his family, he took it and his world changed.

2   *The Notebook*, New Line Cinema, 2004.

At first, everything seemed great—he won fight after fight. Whenever he was tempted to be beaten down, he allowed his mind to slip to the faces of his children and wife, and it gave him the strength to continue winning—all the way up to a showdown with World Heavyweight Champion Max Baer.

Baer, you might remember, was a vicious fighter and was known for killing two men in the ring. A few days before the fight, he ridicules, threatens and mocks Braddock, who begins to get fearful...who begins to forget what got him there...who begins to forget who he is.

When the big day arrives, Braddock's wife sneaks into the bowels of the arena to find her husband in the locker room just moments before the fight. The look in her eyes sends everyone else from the room and she marches straight up to Braddock. With a tender fierceness that can only come from a loyal wife, she locks her husband in her stare for the final words he'll hear before the big event.

"So you just remember who you are," she says. "You're the Bulldog of Bergen and the Pride of New Jersey. You're everybody's hope and the kids' hero. And you are the champion of my heart, James J. Braddock."[3]

Remembering who we are truly makes all the difference. Braddock won the fight.

In some of His final hours with His followers, Jesus called them to come together—to break bread, to drink wine—and to remember Him.[4] Since that time, Christians continue to gather together. It is one of the primary reasons we worship—not just to offer our praise and thanks to Jesus, but to recall the lengths to which He has gone to restore our relationship with Him and reveal His love for us.

So invite this memory before you—whether All Saints' Day in November or any day of the year—invite God to help you remember what He means to you and what you mean to Him. It is God's way of going down into the very heart of our being, of looking us in the eyes and saying, *"Just remember who you are...you are worth more than anything to Me...I brought you into this world because I love you...I redeemed you because I love you...remember you are MY child...you are the champion of my heart...you, my child, are a saint of God..."*

That's a song worth singing.

---

3   *Cinderella Man*, Miramax, 2005.
4   Luke 22:17–20.

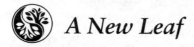

A New Leaf

Do you see yourself as a saint of God? If you are part of the Body of Christ, you are, in fact a saint! My mentor, John Claypool, used to say a sure sign of being a saint is the inner desire to be one. If you have that desire, bring it to Christ...bring it to Him now...and claim your title "Saint of God."

A PRAYER

Almighty God, you have knit together your elect in one communion and fellowship in the mystical body of your Son Christ our Lord. Give us grace so to follow your blessed saints in all virtuous and godly living that we may come to those ineffable joys that you have prepared for those who truly love you; through Jesus Christ our Lord, who with you and the Holy Spirit lives and reigns, one God, in glory everlasting. *Amen.*[5]

---

5   The Collect for All Saints' Day, *The Book of Common Prayer*, p. 245.

Don't Poke the Bear

"Let the peace of Christ rule in your hearts."

— Colossians 3:15

We had a saying where I grew up, "Don't poke the bear." Most bears hibernate, usually beginning when the autumn cold sets in and staying put for up to seven months. Prior to hibernation, of course, bears pack on all the fat they can. They find shelter of some sort, usually a cave, curl into a ball and allow the effects of a slowing metabolism to put them into a deep sleep. It is not uncommon for spelunking humans to come up on a hibernating bear—and while the sleep is deep indeed, the bear can be awakened and let the spelunker beware!

Near my grandmother's house in Blount County, Alabama, there were several small caves on a hill overlooking her house. These were often exploration destinations for my sisters and me. Late one afternoon, my younger sister and I came upon one of these caves— and while too small to crawl into, it was not too narrow to insert the long hiking stick I had brought along. The memory of a low, deep, growl will stay with me for a long time—and I learned the truth of the warning about poking bears!

Humans, particularly those of our time in history, could learn a great deal from hibernating bears. No question that we cannot store up the necessary nutrition to carry us for a seven-month nap; but we could learn that in order to live a balanced life, what is necessary is a wax and wane between movement and stillness, noise and quiet, activity and peace.

Paul and Timothy co-authored the letter to the Christians in Colossae in the early 60s A.D. It is not a long letter, but it was written as an attempt to draw the Colossians away from voices competing for the supremacy of Christ in their lives. In addition, some Colossian Christians were beginning to embrace the early heresy of Gnosticism, of which one of the tenets was it really did not matter what you did with your body, what mattered is your spirit. So it was becoming acceptable, for instance, for some Christians to live morally repugnant lives while at the same time professing an allegiance to Jesus Christ. Such a life, of course, is a divided life—and you and I will remember Jesus' wise counsel that a *"if a house is divided against itself, that house will not be able to stand."*[1]

The counsel of Paul and Timothy was to remove all competing voices and allow Christ to be at the center. That becomes their prayer and want, such that their advice is to, *"Let the peace of Christ rule in your hearts, to which indeed you were called in the one body."*[2]

That is wise counsel for modern Christians as well. There is still much competing for the devotion of our hearts. A few years back, Yankelovich, a marketing research firm, revealed the results of a study which estimated that a person living in a city three decades ago saw about 2,000 advertisements a day (from billboards and road signs to television and magazine ads). But the research went on to suggest that number is close to 5,000 today.[3]

One of the ways Christians have made room for this peace of Christ is to purposely set aside time to, in the words of the psalmist, *"be*

still" and know God.[4] The only way to allow for this kind of spiritual hibernation is to make the time and space for it. We have traditionally called this practice prayer; but essentially, it is any time and any place where we bury all of the voices and visions and thoughts competing for God, and instead give our minds to

1   Mark 3:25.
2   Colossians 3:15.
3   Louise Story, "Anywhere the Eye Can See, It's Likely to See an Ad." *The New York Times*, 15 January, 2007.
4   Psalm 46:10.

Him. Reading this devotional is a form of that, as is reading your Bible. Prayer can be conversation with God using words spoken or thought, or it can be merely silence. We know we are called to this activity, but for some of us (and I have certainly been guilty of this!), it can merely be another item to check off of my to-do list.

The real treasure of spiritual hibernation is intimacy with God. Sue Monk Kidd has suggested, "Intimacy with God does not develop without sacrifice. Mostly it is our reluctance we sacrifice."[5] What keeps us from making this space part of our daily lives is simply activity and we are reluctant to give up something that is an almost constant traveling companion. Yet, as Henri Nouwen wrote, "In solitude, we meet God."[6]

Perhaps it is time to make daily, regular, spiritual hibernation a regular pattern in your life. You choose the place and time of your cave, but when you get there give it the time it deserves—the more you do, the more intimate your experience of God, no question about it. And while you're at it—let it rest—let the peace of Christ become something that is not an occasional visitor, but something that rules in your heart. Oh yes, and don't poke the bear—it needs what it is getting to meet the days to come.

5   Sue Monk Kidd, *God's Joyful Surprise* (New York: HarperOne, 1989), p. 88.
6   Henri Nouwen, *Clowning in Rome* (Garden City, New York: Doubleday, 1979), p. 28.

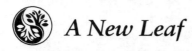 ## A New Leaf

Luke's Gospel tells us that Jesus "would withdraw to deserted places and pray."[7] If it was part of Jesus' practice, should it not be part of yours? Is this practice something you do "often" or just when everything else is checked off the list? Is there anything you can do now to help make more time and space for the peace of Christ to rule in your hearts?

A PRAYER

Lord
Teach me how to still my racing thoughts.
Help me to come to you
arguing nothing,
pleading nothing,
asking nothing,
except to be still
in your presence.
Give me the faith
that will enable me
to lay my burdens at your feet,
and to leave them there
in exchange for the peace
which passes all understanding.[8]
Amen.

— Frank Topping

---

7   Luke 5:16.
8   In *The Doubleday Prayer Collection*, Mary Batchelor, comp. (New York: Doubleday, 1996), pp. 171–172.

Who Gets Your Vote?

"But since we belong to the day, let us be sober,
and put on the breastplate of faith and love,
and for a helmet the hope of salvation."

— I Thessalonians 5:8

The letters of Scripture we know as I and II Thessalonians may be among the oldest of Paul's epistles. Written in the early 50s A.D., Paul and his fellow disciples, Silas and Timothy, write to a Church that Paul founded sometime during his second missionary journey.[1] This letter was written when many of Jesus' followers, including Paul for a season, believed our Lord's return to earth, and the end of the earth as we know it, was imminent. With that in mind, much of what is offered in these two letters is instruction on how to live in the meantime.

Of course not just in this piece of Scripture, but throughout Scripture there is a tension for God's children to live "in this world," but at the same time to be "in God's world." The scripture from I Thessalonians reminds its readers to be cautious about putting too much trust in the way this world runs itself. Paul reminds these early Christians that they are "children of the day," to be self-controlled, to find armor and

1   Acts 17.

protection in faith, love and salvation above and beyond anything the world could offer as protection.

November is voting season in the United States. I have always been an advocate for and participant in the election processes of our nation. What an incredible gift and right it is to have a personal say in the leadership of one's city, state and nation. But you know, like the early Christians, we are "children of the day,"[2] and when it comes to leaders of this world, in whatever fashion they serve, we should never plop all of our eggs in one basket.

Over the years, having lived through several elections now, it has been a fascinating conundrum to witness times when an election draws near and people begin to put a great deal of hope in its outcome. They hope that a particular candidate or party will bring about what we know only God can bring about. They hope that perhaps "this time" the outcome and the new, or next, or renewed, leader will bring one personal happiness. I suppose, with all the energy that goes into those elections, one can certainly understand voters wanting their candidate to bring them joy and satisfaction. But such confidence is misplaced, unrealistic and often a recipe for disappointment.

But there is another path to take toward happiness—unreserved confidence in God. *"Happy are those whose help is the God of Jacob... whose hope is in the Lord their God,"* the psalmist tells us.[3] Better for us to look for happiness in relationship with the Lord God, the one who made heaven and earth, and who is eternally faithful. God is the source of every good and perfect gift, and is a Lord who always keeps promises. With God, we have a leader who can be trusted to provide for us and who never flip-flops. Even more, when we focus on our relationships with God, we find happiness within ourselves.

When we look to God to bring us happiness, we begin to find authentic joy and satisfaction, which secures us even when our leaders disappoint.

Another interesting fallout of election season is that many people believe God is particularly backing one candidate over another. For wisdom there, I'd turn to two of our nation's more well-known leaders. Former Democratic Senator George Mitchell used to quip, "Although He's regularly asked to do so, God does not take sides in American politics." An even wiser word came from our 16th President,

---

2   I Thessalonians 5:5.
3   Psalm 146:5–6.

Republican Abraham Lincoln, who when asked whether or not he believed God was on the side of the Union, President Abraham Lincoln said boldly, "Sir, my concern is not whether God is on our side; my greatest concern is to be on God's side, for God is always right."

The psalmist counseled, *"Do not put your trust in princes, in mortals, in whom there is no help. When their breath departs, they return to the earth; on that very day their plans perish."*[4] This is just another way of saying, remember— when it comes to the ultimate matters of this world, remember you are a "child of the day," and your safety, your security, your joy and satisfaction is found in the protection of God. I'll second that. Who gets your vote?

---

4   Psalm 146:3–4.

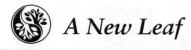 *A New Leaf*

It is responsible citizenship to participate fully in the electoral process. But there is a dividing line between this world and the world of our Lord. You'll recall when Jesus was asked if one should pay taxes to Caesar, His wise response was to yield to Caesar that which is Caesar's, but to God that which is God's.[4] If autumn winds begin to stir your excitement about an upcoming election, there's no harm in that. Just remember Paul's caution—you are a child of the day; then when you do, you can more easily let the chips fall where they may and find your hope, not in a new leader, but in the leadership of your Heavenly Father.

A PRAYER

My Lord God, I have no idea where I am going. I do not see the road ahead of me. I cannot know for certain where it will end. Nor do I really know myself...Therefore I will trust you always though I may seem to be lost and...I will not fear, for you are ever with me, and you will never leave me to face my perils alone. [5] *Amen.*

— Thomas Merton, d. 1968

---

4   Mark 12:13–18.
5   From Thomas Merton, *Thoughts in Solitude* (New York: Farrar, Straus and Giroux, 1958), p. 79.

Every Day Belongs to God

"For everything created by God is good, and nothing is to be rejected, provided it is received with thanksgiving; for it is sanctified by God's word and by prayer."

— I Timothy 4:4–5

Biblical expositors warn preachers like me against something called "proof-texting." Proof-texting is looking into the Bible, grabbing hold of one verse, taking it out of context and using it to prove a point (usually from the point of view of the preacher!). I have done that to some degree throughout this devotional, but I've tried my best to put most of the selected Scriptures within the scope not just of the context of the surrounding verses, but the overall Judeo-Christian story.

But every now and then I come across a verse like this one from I Timothy—and it speaks not just to a particular situation, but to my situation and perhaps to yours, today. The books of I and II Timothy were both written in 63 A.D. from Paul to his protégé, Timothy. They unveil particular guidance for the young man under his tutelage, and if you read them both you can see how much Paul cares for Timothy. Toward the end of

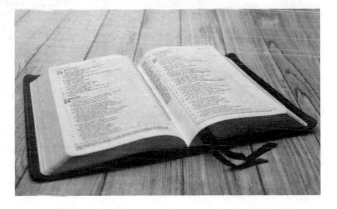

the second epistle, with a kind of loving desperation Paul is spilling out all he can, because—though not written, given the persecutions and martyrdoms of Jesus' early followers—it is clearly implied that Paul may not see Timothy again. These are intimate letters, letters between friends. In them, and through them, Paul wants Timothy to remember some essential truths—one of which is that everything, everything that comes from God, is good. That spoke to me today.

In some ways, it has just been a bad day. Not all days are good days. It was a day when I worked a good deal; it was also a day when I was not at my best. We all have those days. One of the most popular of the late John Denver's songs was "Some Days are Diamonds, Some Days are Stones." The words were actually written by Dick Feller and the chorus goes,

> Some days are diamonds some days are stones
> Sometimes the hard times won't leave me alone
> Sometimes a cold wind blows a chill in my bones
> Some days are diamonds some days are stones.[1]

Does that speak to you? There are days when little things don't go our way—bad traffic, long lines, too many calls to return, a mild cold or stomach bug. There are bigger things—an argument with a loved one, a reprimand from the boss, a child in trouble in school. There are the major ones—a scary diagnosis, a marriage on the rocks, a tragic accident, the death of a friend. As much as we would like to delete these kinds of things from life's inbox, we cannot—they are part of life—as Paul's ominous situation was for his life. And yet...

Yet Paul finds a way to rise above his current circumstances and reminds his young friend that in the midst of things that seem bad, there is always, always something that is good—something that is the fruit of God's creative hand. It may be hard to see, but sometimes you have to look up from your present circumstances.

Every November, usually about the middle of the month, something remarkable happens—it has been happening for as long as history has recorded such things. The earth passes through the trail of the Tempel–Tuttle comet; as a result, the dust left in the wake of this comet produces one of the most spectacular meteor showers of the year. The shower is call the "Leonids" because the orbit of the Tempel–Tuttle comet actually (from our perspective at least) travels through

---

1   First Published performed in 1976, but published and recorded by Denver, RCA Records in 1981.

the constellation of Leo. If you have ever witnessed a meteor shower, it is something otherworldly. Occasionally, most of us have witnessed a meteor as a falling star, when a large piece of rock or ice hits, skims and evaporates across the atmosphere of the earth. But a meteor shower is quite different because the earth is passing through untold numbers of particles. In the case of Leonids, as much as 12 tons of particles are deposited across our planet, resulting in a star shower not to be missed.[2]

Sometimes, we need to be reminded that there is something bigger than our present circumstances. Perhaps God placed meteor showers, and beautiful sunsets, and eclipsing moons and suns, in our skies to help us remember that there is more to life, more to this moment, than meets the eyes.

So when you have a bad day—take heart. God is doing good things all the time—and what is today will not necessarily be tomorrow. More to the point, if you are having a bad day, maybe you'll be reminded that every day belongs to God.

---

2   For the record, it usually begins in mid-November and peaks around November 18.

A New Leaf

In his letter to the Philippians, Paul offered a powerful confession, *"In any and all circumstances I have learned the secret of being well-fed and of going hungry, of having plenty and of being in need. I can do all things through him who strengthens me."*[3] I suppose one could easily respond to Paul, "easier said than done." And yet—how can we contradict a truth which seemed to carry Paul through the exact circumstances he describes? He had been all of those things...and he had been persecuted, physically abused, imprisoned, beaten—in the end, tradition tells us, he was executed outside the walls of Rome. In good times and bad, Paul seems to learn the secret of true contentment—Christ and Christ alone. Don't see Him today? Maybe—maybe go out tonight—open your eyes, open your heart and ask Him to change your point of view.

A PRAYER

Grant to us, O Lord, the royalty of inward happiness, and the serenity which comes from living close to thee. Daily renew in us the sense of joy, and let the eternal Spirit of the Father dwell in our souls and bodies, filling every corner of our hearts with light and grace; so that, bearing about with us the infection of good courage, we may be diffusers of life, and may meet all ills and cross accidents with gallant and high-hearted happiness, giving thee thanks always for all things. *Amen.*

— Robert Louis Stevenson, d. 1894

---

3   Philippians 4:13.

Punching Holes in the Darkness

"What good is it, my brothers and sisters, if you say
you have faith but do not have works? Can faith save
you? If a brother or sister is naked and lacks daily food,
and one of you says to them, 'Go in peace; keep warm
and eat your fill,' and yet you do not supply their bodily
needs, what is the good of that? So faith by itself, if it
has no works, is dead."

— James 2:14–17

Late one fall, I went camping with some of my friends. We were rather deep in the woods, and it was a frigid night. We built a large fire, but could not seem to get warm— so we built it up more, got a bit closer. I remember my feet were growing numb, so I propped them up on the circle of rocks we had used to encircle the flames. I left them there for a while and we got a bit lost in conversation. A little later,

I looked down and the soles of my boots were not only smoking, but they were melting— and my feet were still cold! The boots were ruined, but it was an important lesson in not growing numb to my surroundings.

The Christian faith, as several of these meditations have pointed out, is based on a belief that you and I are made righteous, not by what we do, but by our relationship with our Lord (that works for those we love as well). However, there is the second half of that—if our relationship with Jesus is at the core of who we are then what will flow out of us is caring, loving, righteous actions, not only in our personal mores, but also into the lives of those God sends our way.

That's how it works, certainly, in our closest relationships. If my relationships with my friends were based upon my being the "perfect friend," then those relationships would cease to be. However, because of my affection for my friends, I long to be a good friend not just in word but also in deed. So I stay in touch with my friends, call them, try and remember their birthdays—rejoice when they rejoice, hurt when they hurt, and so on. I don't always get it right, but the friendship does bring about an authentic desire to partner with the life of my friend.

This is, in large part, what the apostle James writes to a rather large Christian audience, those he says are *"in the Dispersion."*[1] Writing around 60 A.D., James no doubt celebrated the good news that our salvation (here and in the life to come) is the result of the work of Christ on the Cross and through the empty tomb. But he lays out an important argument—that good works will follow true faith. True, we Christ-followers are saved not by what we do, but we are, to borrow an old adage, saved to perform good works.[2]

This means, frankly, that it is important that you and I do not grow numb to the needs of God's children around us. Garret Keizer is an Episcopal priest who wrote a little book entitled *A Dresser of Sycamore Trees* in which he addresses this "heaviness" most of us feel when we consider all the challenges the world throws at the human condition. He talks about what he calls "moral obesity." He compared it to a person who sits in front of the television all day eating one bag of chips after another. At the end of the day, they are so full that they can hardly get out of their chair. What he suggests is that it is also possible to become so full and overwhelmed by the darkness of the world that it is literally impossible to know where to begin.[3]

---

1   James 1:1.
2   The full passage runs from James 2:14–26.
3   Garret Keizer, *A Dresser of Sycamore Trees: The Finding of A Ministry* (New York: Viking Press, 1991).

But then, we have friends, this word from James and also Jesus' reminder,

> "for I was hungry and you gave me food, I was thirsty and you gave me something to drink, I was a stranger and you welcomed me, I was naked and you gave me clothing, I was sick and you took care of me, I was in prison and you visited me...Truly I tell you, just as you did it to one of the least of these who are members of my family, you did it to me."[4] And our Lord's brother James, who writes, "Show me your faith apart from your works, and I by my works will show you my faith."[5]

Verses like this tell us there is a "no escape plan" when it comes to reaching out in the name of Jesus Christ to the broken and bruised of this world. And notice, there's no condition put on Jesus' charge, "Feed only the hungry who have tried to get a job...offer something to the thirsty, only if they have sought to find drink for themselves...visit only the unjustly imprisoned..." James does not suggest you only do good deeds to those who will do them in return. No, scripture puts it out there in black and white. When someone in need comes to you, as you are able, reach out, feed, visit, care for, provide.

Now it is possible, as Keizer suggests, that we can become engulfed with the needs around us such that we do not know where to begin. You and I are not called to save the world (that job is taken); but we should be on our guard against being numb to the needs God puts in our path. The best way to address that numbness is to pray—pray that God will send you to those who need you. You don't have to do it all, but you are called to do some—and that some may make all the difference in the world.

A while back, my wife and I spent several days in Edinburgh, Scotland. There was plenty to see, but one afternoon we set out to find the boyhood home of Robert Louis Stevenson. The author of such classics as *Treasure Island* and *Dr. Jekyll and Mr. Hyde*, Stevenson was the son of a well-to-do Presbyterian engineer. Born in 1850, Stevenson had a delicate disposition and his life was fraught with illness. I did not care much about seeing the inside of the home—I only wanted to see its exterior and Heriot Road, which captured the budding author's imagination for so many years. Bedridden for much of his childhood,

---

4   Matthew 25:35–36, 40b.
5   James 2:18b.

the young Stevenson preferred his bed pushed right up to the window so he could watch all the activity on the streets below his room.

One of his favorite parts of the day was sundown. For as dusk settled on the streets of Edinburgh, torchbearers would come by and light the gas street lamps. It is said that this filled the child Robert with such excitement that he would often sit up in bed and say, "Here they come! Here come the ones that punch holes in the darkness!"

No one torchbearer lit all the lights of Edinburgh, but a small army of them certainly did, one by one, and as they did they brought light to the darkened streets. You and I too can be that kind of army—an army of those saved for service, punching holes in the darkness, one life at a time.

A New Leaf

Mother Teresa once wrote, "The poor come to all of us in many forms. Let us be sure that we never turn our backs on them, wherever we may find them. For when we turn our backs on the poor, we turn them on Jesus Christ." Spend a moment in honest prayer—have you grown numb at all to those you encounter, whom you could also serve? What one thing could you begin to do to reveal through your deeds the faith that lives in you?

A PRAYER

Father,
I cannot bring about justice worldwide, but help me to begin
     where I am.
Make me honest and just in all my dealings, true in my words
     and actions.
I cannot alter the course of a suffering and unjust world, but help
me to light candles in the darkness in the name of Jesus Christ, who
will bring the dawn of righteousness and peace at His glorious Day
of Justice and Judgment.[6]
Amen.

— From the Pastoral Team of Bambamarca

---

6   *Vamos Caminando: A Peruvian Catechism / Pastoral Team of Bambamarca*; translated by
     John Medcalf from the Spanish. (London: SCM, 1985).

Angst or Thanks?

"Cast all your anxiety on him, because he cares for you."

— I Peter 5:7

It is natural, I think, when things do not go our way or spin completely out of our control to get anxious and worrisome. It is interesting that one of the Bible passages most often read on Thanksgiving Day comes from Jesus' words in Matthew,

> *"Therefore I tell you, do not worry about your life, what you will eat or what you will drink, or about your body, what you will wear. Is not life more than food, and the body more than clothing? Look at the birds of the air; they neither sow nor reap nor gather into barns, and yet your heavenly Father feeds them. Are you not of more value than they? And can any of you by worrying add a single hour to your span of life?...So do not worry about tomorrow, for tomorrow will bring worries of its own. Today's trouble is enough for today."[1]*

I suppose one reason this lesson is often used on our national holy day of thanks is that it recalls for us a choice made by those who

celebrated the first Thanksgiving. Most of us will remember the story of what our forebears did in 1621. A small group of Puritans set out on the *Mayflower* for Virginia. On their way, they had already endured tremendously high seas and hardship, and were

---

1   Matthew 6:25–27, 34.

eventually blown off course only to land in Cape Cod. The winter ahead of them was horrendous, and by spring only 50 of the original 102 people survived. Many began to discuss that perhaps they should give up hope and go back to the Old World. Their hearty spirits prevailed and they decided instead to stay on and plant corn and barley.

When the anniversary of their landing arrived, discussion arose as to how it should be recognized. Some proposed a day of mourning, when attention would be focused on those who died in the previous year and whose remains were now laying in unmarked graves far away from their original home. But then others suggested something much more profound—a "thanksgiving" for the 50 who survived, the good harvest of their first year's work and befriending the native Americans who could have received them with savagery rather than welcome. It was as if the pilgrims were echoing their understanding from the Gospel lesson this morning. Rather than focusing on what they did not have, they chose to focus on what they had been given by God. Instead of worrying about the things that did not seem to go their way, they chose instead to turn their worry to gratitude.

The apostle Peter suggested something similar in the face of an opportunity to crumble into despair. The books of I and II Peter are written by the apostle upon whom Jesus chose to build His church.[2] But Peter's epistles are written in the 60s A.D.; the second book was written in the late days of that decade, shortly before his execution. At this time in the life of the infant church, the Roman Empire under Emperor Nero had taken persecution to new heights. There was much to bring the heart fear in those dark times, yet Peter encouraged the followers of Jesus Christ scattered throughout portions of Rome to keep their eyes and hearts focused not on the present perils, but on the eternal hope offered in Christ.

Jesus' word about worry was couched not as a suggestion—it is more of a command, *"Do not worry."* Worry creeps in when there is some internal fear that ultimately God is going to pull out the proverbial carpet from under us. But Peter offers an antidote to that worry, *"Cast all your anxiety on him, because he cares for you."*

Peter knew his readers had two choices—to give way to the growing scourge of persecution or to trust in God's love. We have that choice as well when worry raises its ugly head in our own lives. Thomas

2   Matthew 16:13–20; Mark 8:27–29; Luke 9:18–20.

Merton wrote, "Anxiety usually comes from strain, and strain is caused by too complete a dependence on ourselves, on our own devices, our own plans, our own idea of what we are able to do."

Turning from anxiety, fear and worry to God is merely an act of faith, of trust. It is not so much about getting control over a situation, but instead turning that control over to God—that too can be a fearful thing, but it really is the only way to assuage the disquiet within us.

So, as those early pilgrims did, may November's Thanksgiving be an invitation to you to turn your angst into thanks and find your way to easing your worries—because He does care for you, He does indeed.

 ## A New Leaf

George Müller was a minister and evangelist who lived a long full life—taking on and mending the suffering of much of his world by caring for and tending to orphaned children. He once wrote, "The beginning of anxiety is the end of faith, and the beginning of true faith is the end of anxiety."[3] Can I invite you to put it out there? About what are you anxious today? Lay this before our Lord—tell Him your troubles—let His love soothe your angst away and in its place create a grateful heart.

---

3   Müller was born in Germany and died in Bristol, England in 1898.

A PRAYER

Now thank we all our God,
with heart, and hands and voices,
who wondrous things hath done,
in whom his world rejoices;
who from our mothers' arms
has blessed us on our way
with countless gifts of love,
and still is ours today.

O may this bounteous God
through all our life be near us!
with ever-joyful hearts
and blessed peace to cheer us;
and keep us in his grace,
and guide us when perplexed,
and free us from all ills
in this world and the next.

All praise and thanks to God
the Father now be given,
the Son, and him who reigns
with them in highest heaven,
eternal, Triune God,
whom earth and Heaven adore;
for thus it was, is now,
and shall be, evermore. [4]
Amen.

—Martin Rinckart, d. 1649

---

4   Martin Rinckart (d. 1649). From *The Hymnal 1982* (New York: The Church Pension Fund, 1985), #396.

Martin Rinckart was a Lutheran Clergyman who served in Eilenburg, Germany. In 1636, amid the darkness of the Thirty Years War, Martin Rinkart is said to have buried 5,000 parishioners in a year, an average of 15 a day. It was in the midst of this war, death and economic disaster that he sat down and wrote a table grace for his children, which has been adapted as the beautiful prayer into a hymn often sung in churches on Thanksgiving Day.

What Remains

"Beloved, let us love one another, because love is from God; everyone who loves is born of God and knows God...God is love, and those who abide in love abide in God, and God abides in them...We love because he first loved us...The commandment we have from him is this: those who love God must love their brothers and sisters also."

— I John 4:7, 16, 19, 21

When autumn has finished its days and begins to turn to winter, the leaves have fallen, have been raked away, and only the bare trunks

and branches remain. Without them, we would have beauty in no season. Nourished by their unseen roots, these are the visible arms of nature from which life returns when the cold days pass away. No trunks, no branches, no leaves, no photosynthesis—*no life*.

Our Christian life is like that. When it is stripped bare, only one thing remains—God. God, John writes, is love. It is possible to have all kinds of Christian attributes, but they are empty without the One who is love, embodies love.

John's three epistles were written well beyond the time frame of most of the New Testament, from the early 90s A.D. and beyond. While he includes a great deal of reflection and instruction, unlike the other letters, there is no specific greeting or recipient. But what the reader will find is his continued focus throughout on the call to love. For this reason, John is often called "The Apostle of Love."[1]

What does that mean for you and me? It means what it says...if we are followers of Jesus Christ, then we cannot check the "opt out" box when it comes to loving those around us. Some years ago, I read an article by a man who became an important friend and mentor in my life—the Anglican priest, preacher and theologian, John Stott.

In the article, John referred to love as an "unforbidden fruit." Playing a bit off of Paul's famous "Love Chapter" in I Corinthians, John made several key points. He rightly noted that people have a wide variety about the hallmark of being a follower of Christ. When asked what is the chief distinguishing mark of the child of God, some reply "Truth, orthodoxy, submission to the authority of the Scriptures, the Creeds or the Articles of Faith." To some degree, of course, they are right. Revealed truth is vital. Submission to the Scriptures is crucial. Our Christian heritage springs from a rich history and story of revelation, tradition and Spirit-led reason.

But recall that wonderful bit of Scripture from Paul's first letter to the Corinthians in 13:2, that we often hear at weddings, *"If I...understand all mysteries and all knowledge...but do not have love, I am nothing."*[2]

Some believe that the true mark of a believer is faith because we are justified by faith alone through grace alone—and this, too, is true. Yet Paul writes, *"If I have all faith, so as to remove mountains, but do not have love, I am nothing."*[3]

Others believe the essential characteristic of the Christian is religious experience, perhaps an experience of a particular emotional and vivid kind, which they sometimes insist everyone must have. Of course, religious experience is important. Nevertheless, Paul writes, *"If I speak in the tongues of mortals and of angels, but do not have love, I am a noisy gong or clanging cymbal."*[4]

Certainly those among us who are more socially inclined will say the *real* Christian faith is evidenced in our service to others. In a large part, these folk too, are right. James warned that without

---

1   This is the same author of the Gospel of John and the book of Revelation. He is referred to in John's Gospel as *"the disciple whom Jesus loved."* (13:23) Not that Jesus did not love all of His disciples; but He did, in fact, clearly have a unique affinity for John and at the end of His life, Jesus entrusted His mother Mary to John's care. (19:25–27)

2   I Corinthians 13:2

3   I Corinthians 13:2

4   I Corinthians 13:1

the good works of love, service and charity, our faith is dead. But again Paul warns, *"If I give away all my possessions, and if I hand over my body so that I may boast, but do not have love, I gain nothing."*[5]

Above all of the possible characteristics of the Christian life and ministry is love. *Love is the authentic mark of the Christian.* Stott concluded the article by affirming that we need doctrine, that faith is essential, religious experience is important and Christian deeds are necessary—but he pointed out that in the end, when all is said and done Jesus said, *"By this everyone will know that you are my disciples, if you have love for one another."*[6, 7]

John's assertion that *"we love because He first loved us"* also tells us how to be the disciples of love we are called to be—by receiving God's love for us. For all kinds of reasons, many people either do not know they are loved, or forget they are loved, or have never even experienced authentic love. But when one opens his or her heart and sees what God sees—the object of His divine love—then true love is not just a source of healing for the unloved one but also an inspiration for that person to love others.

The late Archbishop of Canterbury, William Temple, wrote, "Love of God is the root, love of our neighbor the fruit of the Tree of Life. Neither can exist without the other, but the one is cause and the other effect."

So then, let the bare trees of late autumn remind you—when all that comes with church, and Christianity, and religion for that matter—when all is stripped away, what remains is God, what remains is love. Indeed, we love because He first loved us; love one another; by this, everyone will know you are a disciple of Jesus Christ, if you have love for one another.

---

5   I Corinthians 13:2–3.
6   John 13:35.
7   John Stott, "The Unforbidden Fruit," in *Christianity Today*. August, 1992, p. 34.

 *A New Leaf*

Do you know you are loved? Loved by God? St. Augustine wrote, "He who is filled with love is filled with God Himself." Can you open your heart to that love today? And as you do, so filled, can you with God's help love all who come your way? Look for new ways to love this day. Ask God to send others to you—this day—who need to be touched by His love through you.

A Prayer

Lord Jesus,
Your beloved disciple John wrote that perfect love casts out all fear.
Give me and fill me with that love,
thus being free from fear of loving others,
I may open wide my arms and heart...
...loving as You have loved me.
For Your sake, by Your Power, and in Your Name,
    Love incarnate, God Almighty.
Amen.

King Me!

"Now to him who is able to keep you from falling, and
to make you stand without blemish in the presence of his
glory with rejoicing, to the only God our Savior, through
Jesus Christ our Lord, be glory, majesty, power, and
authority, before all time and now and forever. Amen."

— Jude 24–25

Jude, the next to last book in the New Testament, was written in the early 80s A.D. by the author of the same name, who might have been one of Jesus' brothers.[1] His recipient was every follower of Jesus and his full purpose was to remind them—again and again—to persevere in allowing Jesus to be their Lord, their Savior—their King. So, he ends the letter with several glorious adjectives fit, we might say, for a king.

The last Sunday before Advent, and thus the last Sunday of November, is recognized throughout the Church as "Christ the King" Sunday. It is a day we hold up the Christ as our King—the ultimate power not just in our lives, but in all creation. We need to remember that because we often replace our Monarch by relinquishing our lives to other kinds of powers.

Power is an interesting quality. It is almost tangible. Usually, when we think we really have power, we feel pretty good...in control. When we are on the other end of it, we feel not so good.

That said, we are living through an interesting time that cultural sociologist are call "post-modern," meaning that many of the avenues of power, for good or ill, in which people have trusted to bring them a feeling of security have failed, or at the very least disappointed.

---

1   See Matthew 13:55, Mark 6:3.

Living near College Station, Texas, I have frequented the George H.W. Bush Presidential Library. I certainly commend it to you for many reasons, but one of the most striking, poignant icons that offers a vision into another world is a large piece of the wall that separated East and West Germany. It is a visible reminder that fascism and communism did not hold the answers many once believed they did. Those who believe, and some as we know do, that socialism may hold the answer for humanity have to admit the huge gaps that ideology leaves in an ordered society. And if we are honest, we must confess even capitalism has its flaws.

The industrial revolution did great things, but left us with pollution. The nuclear age brought us far, but left us with the threat of annihilation. The computer/scientific age excites us, but also seems to probe us to ask whether we have gone too far. Neither the European Union nor its euro are the economic magic formula many thought they might be. All of these have still left humanity with an abiding sense of unfulfillment and dissatisfaction. Things that, and people who, seem to have the power to give us an abiding sense of what we really want or need, fail us time and time again.

The Bible tells us that power, real power, does not come from the inside out, but from the outside in; not from the human side of the equation, but from another side. It says that real power, enduring power, is not something one can accomplish, but instead can only receive.

Paul wrote to the Church in Ephesus,

> *"I pray that..., with the eyes of your heart enlightened, you may know what is the hope to which he has called you, what are the riches of his glorious inheritance among the saints, and what is the immeasurable greatness of his power for us who believe, according to the working of his great power. God put this power to work in Christ when he raised him from the dead and seated him at his right hand in the heavenly places, far above all rule and authority and power and dominion, and above every name that is named, not only in this age but also in the age to come. And he has put all things under his feet and has made him the head over all things for the church, which is his body, the fullness of him who fills all in all."[2]*

To paraphrase Paul, **if you are looking for power—power to live this life, to endure this life, to make it through this life—it is found in Jesus Christ.**

If there is, in fact, no perfect "ism," politician or leader; and if there nothing on the "inside" that can bring us the kind of enduring gifts we need—things like forgiveness, mercy, grace, hope, faith—things that can only be received and not achieved, if we can admit this then we can also have the humility to confess what Paul tells us—that the power we crave, the power we need, comes from only one place... only one person...Christ.

The point, the goal if you will, of thinking on the Kingship of Christ is to recall for us just who Christ is— King of creation. In doing so, if He is not yet King, or we have tossed Him off the throne of our hearts, we have the opportunity to re-throne Him by allowing Him to be King yet again, and you, a grateful subject.

I don't know if you are a checker player, but if you know the game,

---

2   Ephesians 1:18–22.

the only way to win back pieces you have lost is to get all the way to the opposite side of the board...at that point, you say "King me!" And when you say "King me," your opponent gives you back what you lost, and you now have the power to move in any direction you want!

One of the real joys of knowing who is your boss is giving over your power to him or her. Our story, your story and mine, says that when we turn our lives over to Christ, we get something only He can give. It is only when we lose ourselves to Him that we find we can live with a kind of freedom that we have never before had. That, my friends, is peace...and peace is the *only real power that endures*.

Perhaps it is time to say with Jude, *"To the only God, our Savior...be glory, majesty, power, and authority."* Or more to the point, just turn your eyes and heart to Jesus and say, "King me!"

 ## A New Leaf

Is Jesus your King? Or is there something else, someone else, who has taken His proper place on that throne in your heart? Let it come to mind. It is so tempting to hold onto those things, those other alluring powers, whatever they may be, and believe that they hold some kind of real power for us. But the only real power is in losing every other competing king, all those kings of our making—losing them all—losing them all to Christ.

Want power, real power? Know how to get there? Lose...lose it all. And then, with great abandon, open your arms, your life, your heart—and say with all that you are "King me! King me!" And then wander joyfully and peacefully over the board of life, living as Christ means for you to live—a life of *"the immeasurable greatness of his power for us who believe."*

A Prayer

Now it is You alone that I love,
You alone that I follow,
You alone that I seek,
You alone that I feel ready to serve,
Because You alone rule justly.
It is to Your authority alone that I want to submit.
Command me, I pray, to do whatever You will,
but heal and open my ears
that I may hear your voice.
Heal and open my eyes
that I may see Your will.
Drive out from me
all fickleness,
that I may acknowledge You alone.
Tell me where to look
that I may see You,
and I will place my hope in doing Your will.
Amen.

—St. Augustine, d. 430

The Beginning at the End

"See, I am coming soon; my reward is with me, to repay according to everyone's work. I am the Alpha and the Omega, the first and the last, the beginning and the end."

— Revelation 22:12–13

Of all the books in Holy Scripture, Revelation is perhaps the most unusual. Scholars put its writing as early as Nero's reign (54–68 A.D.) and as late as the reign of Domitian (81–96 A.D.). Written by the Apostle John, it is a long letter of sorts—a collection of words and visions from Jesus to John during his exile on the Island of Patmos.[1]

Clearly, it was written in a time when Christian persecution was growing stronger (which would have been true under Nero or Domitian). The Roman state was enforcing emperor worship and Christians who were firm to the end could not offer their allegiance to Caesar over Christ.

As the last book of the Bible, and according to John the last written revelation of God, its theme is about the end of times and how to persevere and remain strong in the meantime.[2] There are visions, symbols and metaphors that are hard to understand fully. The book itself has been over-interpreted and under-interpreted. Some parts perhaps should be taken literally (such as Jesus' words to the Seven Churches in Chapters 2–3), but much is to be taken as symbolism,

---

1   Revelation 1:9.
2   In 22:18–19, John writes, *"I warn everyone who hears the words of the prophecy of this book: if anyone adds to them, God will add to that person the plagues described in this book; if anyone takes away from the words of the book of this prophecy, God will take away that person's share in the tree of life and in the holy city, which are described in this book."* The suggestion is not that God had ended his self-revelation in any form (written, verbal or otherwise), but that this represented the end of what is revealed through Holy Scripture.

thoughts offered in human words and visions so we could better understand the unfathomable.

Suffice it to say, as it brings a close to Holy Scripture, it is clear that our Lord's word to the human family is this: when the end comes it is not the end, but only a new beginning.

So let me bring this collection of autumn meditations to a close with a focus on the new beginning we face when death comes—let me unpack for a moment some thoughts on heaven and afterlife.

I'll start by quoting C.S. Lewis again, who wrote in his book, *The Problem of Pain,*

> We are very shy nowadays of even mentioning Heaven. We are afraid of the jeer about "pie in the sky," and of being told that we are trying to "escape from the duty of making a happy world here and now into dreams of a happy world elsewhere." But either there is "pie in the sky" or there is not. If there is not, then Christianity is false, for this doctrine is woven into its whole fabric. If there is, then this truth, like any other, must be faced...We are afraid that heaven is a bride, and that if we make it our goal we shall no longer be disinterested. It is not so. Heaven offers nothing that a mercenary soul can desire. It is safe to tell the pure in heart that they shall see God, for only the pure in heart want to.[3]

For the purposes of closure, I'm going to make two assumptions. The first is that there is life after death for those who follow and give their lives to our Lord. The second is that we know something about that life, but are far from knowing everything.

All of us have questions about life after death. While Christians do believe in the promises of our Lord that His followers will indeed experience life after death, some may still be asking, "What *kind of life* is there after death?"

To begin answering that question, I have to utter four very honest words, "I do not know." The apostle Paul shared a word about his own ignorance on this question when he wrote to the church in Corinth, *"For now we see in a mirror, dimly, but then we will see face to face. Now I know only in part; then I will know fully, even as I have been fully known."*[4]

---

3   C.S. Lewis, *The Problem of Pain* (New York: HarperOne, 1940), pp. 148-149.
4   I Corinthians 13:12.

I believe we see glimpses behind death's door throughout Holy Scripture. Consider the scene from the Transfiguration in which Jesus is visited by what appears to be Moses and Elijah.[5] In this visitation, the visitors are recognized and even speak with Jesus. When Jesus rises from the grave, He appears to Mary Magdalene, who first recognizes Jesus' voice and then his face.[6]

Jesus also appears to the disciples and even invites the doubting Thomas to touch him.[7] Later, Jesus visits with them, eats with them and I can only imagine that he also laughed with them![8] We are told in Luke's sequel, the book of Acts, that resurrected Jesus walked the earth for about 40 days, continuing His work of sharing the Good News of the Kingdom.[9]

Then again, remember, Jesus' risen body was not a medically resuscitated one. It did not come to life as a result of an injection of adrenaline and a jolt of electricity from a defibrillator. The power of God did this. The resurrected body that contained Jesus on earth had been transformed in a way that expressed that very power. We still do not see that type of resurrection in our day-to-day lives; so the question remains, "What kind of life is there after death?"

I think these appearances tell us just a few clear things:

First, that we will remain who we are—God created us as unique beings and we will but only die once.[10] Thus, we will not be reincarnated. We will move from this life to the next and continue in God's kingdom.

Second, we do not become angels either. Angels are heavenly beings created by God to assist God in God's work. Humans, we are told, are greater than angels and, by the way, we are also told that sometimes we entertain them without knowing it![11]

Lastly, there is still much mystery about what rests after death! But the certainty to which Christians cling is the certainty that for those who trust in the Lordship of Jesus Christ, and surrender to His grace and mercy, that death is merely a moment that opens the door to eternal life.

5   Matthew 17:1–13 and Mark 9:2–13
6   John 20:10ff.
7   John 20:24ff.
8   John 21:12–15.
9   Acts 1:1–5.
10   Hebrews 9:27.
11   Psalm 8:5, Hebrews 2:7 and 13:2.

This I *do* know—it is ultimately a matter of trust. We find that hard these days because we so often want to know the whys and hows about everything. Modern humans sometimes have trouble with unanswered questions and unsolved mysteries. Parker Palmer in

his little book, *Let Your Life Speak*, notes this cultural trend writing, "...our culture wants to turn mysteries into puzzles to be explained or problems to be solved, because maintaining the illusion that we can 'straighten things out' makes us feel powerful. Yet mysteries never yield to solutions or fixes—and when we pretend that they do, life becomes not only more banal but also more hopeless, because the fixes never work."[12]

John Claypool used to say to me all the time, "When my life is over, if there is anything else, it's up to God." That is a powerful statement not only of fact, but of faith.

If someone were to have told me in the comfort of my mother's womb that I should jump from a luxury hotel with 24-room service into a bed and breakfast where I would begin with a slap on the bum, a limited menu, a life that included eating, breathing and communicating in a way I could not at that point understand, I would have said, "No way! I'm fine just where I am!" Now that I am here, I would never choose to go back to the womb. Christianity tells us that there is indeed something even greater waiting past the door of death. I wish I had more evidence of what it really is like, but my guess is that when I get there, I will never want to come back here.

Perhaps a story, the late, great, chaplain of the United States Senate Peter Marshall used to tell will offer an image worth clinging to as we ponder our own deaths.

It seems a mother in a church where he was serving had a young son who had succumbed to the ravages of leukemia. As his body weakened, their greatest joy was to spend afternoons with her reading

12   Parker Palmer, *Let Your Life Speak* (San Francisco: Jossey-Bass, 1999) p. 60.

stories to him—particularly those of the Camelot and the Knights of the Round Table.

As she read about one particular battle scene, her son looked at her with a childlike innocence and said, "Mom, what is it like to die?" She knew that he was not asking about the story—he was asking about himself. He was asking the same question many of us innocently ask.

Marshall said that the woman was so overcome with emotion that she paused, closed the book, and looked at her beloved son. She told him she would be back in a minute and excused herself. She went out into the kitchen, knelt on the floor and literally prayed—asking God to give her an answer to her son's almost unanswerable question. She opened her eyes and lifted her head, and as she did, her eyes lit upon a photo of her older son tacked on the refrigerator—and she was given her answer.

She went out, sat next to her son and said, "You just asked me what happens when you die. Well son, I have not died, so I do not know. But I have to believe it is something like this.

"Do you remember back when you were more healthy...you could run and play in the afternoons? Some of those days you would come in and plop down on the sofa; you were often so tired that you would fall asleep in front of the television. Some nights, I just did not have the heart to wake you and so I would ask your older brother to pick you up and take you to your room.

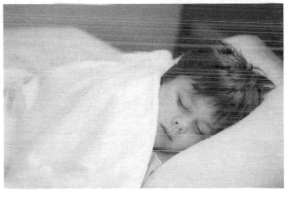

"The next morning, you would wake—not in your old clothes, but in your clean pajamas—in your own bed. You did not know how you got there, but all that happened is you went to sleep in this room of your father's house and you woke in another. That is what I believe it is like for the children of God," his mother said.

What a wonderful truth this mother spoke to her child at the end of this life's journey! We know that summer gives way to autumn, and autumn gives way to something that looks pretty much like the end of all things. But soon, for lots of reasons—soil, sun, water, nourishment—the end will begin again. What looked to be death was actually just life preparing itself for new life—again.

So in the end, if there is anything more after death, it *is* up to God. Our faith proclaims there is. Knowing God as I do, I believe that it will be better than we could ever ask or imagine. Indeed, *"Whoever believes in Him may have eternal life."*[13] This is one of the many reasons we call our faith Good News—for it is good news indeed that what Jesus offers His followers is the promise that at death, life is changed, not ended. And that beyond death's door we will be welcomed by His words, *"Come, you that are blessed by my Father, inherit the kingdom prepared for you from the foundation of the world."*[14] That is...Good News...indeed!

 ## A New Leaf

Take some time today to ponder the end of things. These lives of ours will not last forever, yet our story offers hope. It is not a clock or calendar that rules time, but God, who is the Alpha and the Omega, and the testimony of Scripture. Our Christian faith is that when things, when death, when lives are placed in His hands, the words "The End" never roll across the screen. In the midst of winter—wait—spring comes again.

---

13 John 3:15.
14 Matthew 25:34.

A Prayer

Love divine, all loves excelling,
Joy of heaven, to earth come down;
Fix in us Thy humble dwelling;
All Thy faithful mercies crown.
Jesus, Thou art all compassion,
Pure, unbounded love Thou art;
Visit us with Thy salvation;
Enter every trembling heart.
Breathe, O breathe Thy loving Spirit

Into every troubled breast!
Let us all in Thee inherit,
Let us find the promised rest;
Take away our bent to sinning;
Alpha and Omega be;
End of faith, as its beginning,
Set our hearts at liberty.

Come, Almighty to deliver,
Let us all Thy grace receive;
Suddenly return, and never,
Never more Thy temples leave.
Thee we would be always blessing,
Serve Thee as Thy hosts above,
Pray, and praise Thee without ceasing,
Glory in Thy perfect love.

Finish, then, Thy new creation;
Pure and spotless let us be;
Let us see Thy great salvation
Perfectly restored in Thee;
Changed from glory into glory,
Till in heaven we take our place,
Till we cast our crowns before Thee,
Lost in wonder, love, and praise.
Amen.[15]

---

15   Charles Wesley (d. 1788). From the *Baptist Hymnal* (Nashville, Tennessee: Convention Press, 1956), #2.

Pregnant Pause

"One thing I do know, that though I was blind, now I see."

— John 9:25

I love this scene in John's Gospel. A blind man is healed by Jesus. When the religionists begin to investigate this miracle, they interrogate the blind man trying to find some kind of answer that will help nail

Jesus to the cross (literally). But, when push came to shove, the only answer the man could give was, "You know, I can't explain it other than to tell you I was blind and now I see!"

If you have made it to the end of this little book, I offer my gratitude to a patient reader. I hope it has been helpful in your journey with our Lord. Maybe you have walked with Him your whole life through. Maybe you came alongside Jesus at a particular moment in life. Maybe this book has helped you take that kind of step—perhaps you are still holding it all at arm's length.

The reason I like the story of the blind man healed by Jesus is I can really identify with him. There is a lot—so very much—I do not know about our faith. I know some things, some come from years of study—directed and personal; a great deal comes from decades of experience as a priest and pastor; but there is still much I don't know. This I do know; however, the more I entrust my life to Jesus Christ, the more I see, the more I am healed, the more life becomes real, deeper and fuller.

I am not one who believes a Christian's life is without troubles and woes; you only have to look at the lives of Jesus' first Apostles to know that is true. But I do believe that life with Him is better than life without Him—in fact, really to buy into that is to not buy into life at all. Jesus said He came to give us both abundant life here and eternal life beyond the grave.[1] That alone is enough to give one's life to our Lord.

So wherever you are in your journey, I pray that as you have turned over the leaves of this book, that it has been helpful in guiding you more fully to the hope there is in Christ. If you have been using it, as intended, as a companion through the autumn season, remember that winter will come, but then there is spring—and life begins again.

Soon, only days away really, we will begin to reflect again on young Mary to whom the angel came and invited her to bear God's Son. I suppose, though clearly chosen by God, Mary could have turned away from the offer to bring Love Incarnate into the world through her womb. But, she did not—having heard God's invitation, her response was *"Here am I, the servant of the Lord; let it be with me according to your word."*[2]

We sometimes use the two words "pregnant pause" to indicate a full stop in whatever is going on—allowing for a silence full of meaning.

Let me invite you, as you close this book, to that kind of pause today. If you have given your life to our Lord—then give Him thanks. If you have stepped away from a faith that has nourished you at another season in your life, well then, consider coming back to that wellspring from which you once were nourished.

And, if you have yet to give your life to Jesus, may I invite you to drop your stiffened arm and invite Him to embrace you with His grace, His love and mercy. It will be the beginning of a new day, a new life, a new season—that will, indeed, last forever.

---

1   John 10:10; John 11:25-26.
2   Luke 1:38.

A PRAYER

Lord Jesus,
I commend to You my life—
all that I am, all that I have;
all that has been, is, and will be,
I give to You.

Take my darkest places and forgive them.
Take my broken places and heal them.
Take my empty places and fill them.

I give You my hopes, that they may be fulfilled.
I give You my joy, that it may increase.
I give You my bliss, that it may be perfected in You.

I give You my life, my life Lord...
here it is...it is now Yours...
so that in You and through You,
I can be who You created me to be,
and in life, and in death, and in life to come...
        I can finally rest, in Your everlasting peace.
Amen.

Scripture Index

Author Index

Other Books

BY THIS AUTHOR

Preparing Room – A Collection of Scriptures, Meditations and Prayers by Russell J. Levenson, Jr.

AN ADVENT COMPANION

"Russ Levenson wants faith to connect to living. His Lent book was a tour de force – connected and powerful. I am sure that anyone reading and using this Advent book will find their walk a little bit closer to Jesus – the one we anticipate this season."

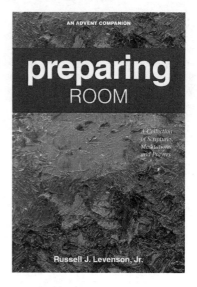

> – The Very Reverend Dr. Ian Markham, Dean and President of Virginia Theological Seminary

"This new book of his, Preparing Room, because it is packed full of powerful Scriptures, prayers and teachings, has already impacted my life at my first reading! Great teaching is added to the scripture. The prayers are life-giving. God's hand was on Russell's as this was written. I believe that firmly."

> – Lani Netter, President, Lani Netter Productions and Co-Producer, with her husband, Academy Award Winning Producer Gil Netter, on the film *The Shack,* based on the best-selling book

"Preparing Room is an important resource for Advent with its practical, realistic, and live-giving assurance of God's Grace for all through the gift of the world of Jesus Christ."

> – Dr. Neal R. Berte, President Emeritus, Birmingham Southern College

"Dr. Levenson is not only insightful and wise, but also humorous. He presents a realistic approach to biblical stories that other people often 'dress up' or sugarcoat. I highly recommend this book that provided both a compelling challenge and comfort for our benefit, while bidding us to open our hearts and lives to God."

> – Ann Claypool Beard, LCSW, Editor of "The First to Follow: The Apostles of Jesus," compiled from recordings by her late husband, the Rev. Dr. John Claypool, beloved Episcopal priest and author

Provoking Thoughts – A Collection of Scriptures, Meditations and Prayers by Russell J. Levenson, Jr.

A Lenten Companion

"Dr. Levenson does not duck the tough questions as some preachers tend to do, neither does he offer simplistic solutions to the moral demands that come our way day after day. Instead, he reminds us why being a Christian is the most wonderful thing in the whole world."

> — The Most Reverend and Right Honorable Dr. George L. Carey 103rd Archbishop of Canterbury

"Although it is technically a book for Lent, Provoking Thoughts is a life-saver for any season where we want to personally experience the life-changing love and grace we can only receive through God and his son Jesus. It miraculously helps us hear in the clearest voice, 'Be still, and know that I am God.'"

> — Micheal Flaherty, Co-Founder, Walden Media, President, Good Thief Productions, and Producer of *The Chronicles of Narnia*, *Amazing Grace* and *The Giver*

"One definition of 'provoke' is to inflame, and that is just what this beautifully written book of Lenten meditations does. It sets the love of God ablaze in our hearts, tilting us toward disciplined devotion on the way to Holy Week and Victory Sunday at Easter morn."

> — Timothy George, Founding Dean, Beeson Divinity School of Samford University and General Editor, Reformation Commentary on Scripture

"It takes a gifted writer to inspire and challenge, to encourage and confront, all at the same time. Dr. Levenson does just that with his Lenten devotional. Provoking Thoughts engages the mind, touches the heart, and draws us into a closer relationship with God, through our savior Jesus Christ."

> — Rob Pearigen, President, Millsaps College

Summer Times – A Collection of Scriptures, Meditations and Prayers by Russell J. Levenson, Jr.

A SUMMER COMPANION

"The traditional Anglican term for the days and weeks of summer is 'Ordinary Time,' but this small but potent book is anything but. It is an extraordinary gift to all of us from Russ Levenson, priest and pastor."

> — Jon Meacham, Former Editor and Chief of *Newsweek* and Executive Editor and Executive Vice President of Random House

"My friend Russ Levenson invites us to pause and ponder the gladness of God. His words are like his heart: winsome and gracious. Let him lead you into a quiet place where you will receive a gentle touch from your heavenly Father."

> — Max Lucado, Senior Pastor of Oak Hills Church, San Antonio

"In this wonderful, refreshing, and powerful book, an experienced Rector holds your hand and takes you through the eternal truths that can shape and enhance a life. With humor and anecdote, he helps you understand the gift of faith. As you plan your summer, this is a must read addition. With this book, Russ Levenson is becoming the finest writer of devotional texts in the Episcopal Church today."

> — The Very Reverend Ian Markham, Dean and President of Virginia Theological Seminary

AN ADVENT WREATH DEVOTIONAL

by Laura and Russell J. Levenson, Jr.

With this devotional, we hope to provide you with a framework to travel within the circle of God's love throughout the Advent season. Using a question, some Scripture, a brief meditation and a closing prayer, we will offer you what we hope will be a regular companion in your Advent journey for years to come.

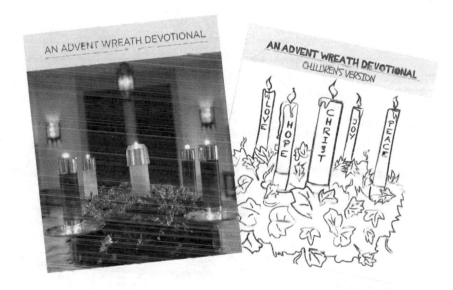